BLOOD WARNING

Also by John Dillmann

Unholy Matrimony
The French Quarter Killers

≡ BLOOD ≡ WARNING

JOHN DILLMANN

G. P. PUTNAM'S SONS
New York

To my parents,
John and Beverly Dillmann,
and my sister,
Karon Dillmann Borrego

G. P. Putnam's Sons
Publishers Since 1838
200 Madison Avenue
New York, NY 10016

Library of Congress Cataloging-in-Publication Data

Dillmann, John.
Blood warning / John Dillmann.
p. cm.
1. Murder—Louisiana—New Orleans—Case studies. 2. Homicide
investigation—Louisiana—New Orleans—Case studies. 3. Vieux Carré
(New Orleans, La.) I. Title.
HV6534.N45D54 1989   89-3995 CIP
364.1'523 0976335—dc20

ISBN 0-399-13485-9

Printed in the United States of America
2   3   4   5   6   7   8   9   10

Acknowledgments

I wish to thank Michael Rice and my closest friend, Fred Dantagnan. Without their help this case might never have been solved, and this book might never have become a reality.

Special thanks to members of the NOPD Homicide Division, and to all my brother officers. After three years I still miss them and think about them daily.

I would like to acknowledge my family—Diane, Todd, and Amy; Don and Linda Guillot; all my friends at Dillmann/Guillot Associates; David Plavnicky; Walter Sentenn; and Judge Jerome Winsberg.

I also thank my editor, Lisa Wager, whose hard work and sharp pencil contributed greatly to this book.

And others deserve gratitude: Judy Hoffman; William III, Joe, Terri, and John Hoffman; Lisa Schaffer; Alicia, Ethan, and Micah Lewis; John and Anita Reeves; Leonard and Bess McBrayer; Margaret Wood; Ola Graney; Joe and Linda Lewandoski; Jess Jensen; Jeanne Schorr; Jerry Shields; L. D. Shank; Dwight and Barbara Steward; Charles Ced; Rudy Ced; Betty Duke; Kim Blackledge; James and Johnnie Sue Blackledge; Mo and Patricia Reich; James and Donna Cherrier; and William Hoffman, Sr., and Anna Hoffman.

≡1≡

"**S**ignal Thirty." The voice of Homicide Supervisor Paul Drouant crackled over the car radio. "Meet a First District unit at 629 Governor Nicholls." Signal 30 means murder.

The call came at 1:35 P.M., Wednesday, November 26, 1980, the day before Thanksgiving, as Detective Dantagnan and I rode in our unmarked white Ford along New Orleans's Lakeshore Drive, admiring the sailboats on Lake Pontchartrain. We'd just finished working one murder—Fred handled the investigation, I'd gone along to assist—when headquarters radioed for me.

"I'll notify backup units," Drouant intoned, "to join you at the scene."

Adrenaline started pumping, as always, nerve endings tingled and my stomach churned, suddenly bathed with acid.

In reflective moments some homicide detectives compare themselves to football placekickers, players who seldom see game action except in critical situations. Just so, killings do not occur all the time, though recently it seemed they did.

Like a placekicker's, my number had come up. I was being called to perform the way training and experience taught me.

Dealing with murder never failed to set me on edge. The time for a homicide detective to transfer or retire comes when he gets used to murder. The way I was feeling told me I had a long way to go before I got accustomed to killings.

Unspoken thoughts ran through my mind. What type of murder awaited on Governor Nicholls? An old man pulled from the river? A child beaten to death? *Whose* life had ended—and why?

"What is this, the preholiday rush?" Fred groused.

It had already been a busy day for the death squad when our drive by the lake on the way back to headquarters became a detour from one murder to another. We'd just left a "clean" one—a man killed in a bar—to head for a second so grisly even veteran uniforms averted their eyes.

Governor Nicholls, an old, narrow road built for horses and buggies, allowed no on-street parking. We spotted several blue-and-white units, lights flashing, blocking traffic. I pulled the plainclothes car onto the sidewalk a block away, then Fred and I walked along the cozy one-way street, its stately nineteenth-century homes converted into apartment houses.

The Indian-summer day was sunny and warm, with nothing in the air to suggest the macabre scene we were about to enter. Fred and I toted the tools of our trade: clipboards, briefcases packed with tape measures, assorted envelopes to hold evidence, plastic bags, surgical gloves, Lysol spray to combat overpowering odor, and coffee grounds we'd ignite in a saucer to burn off insufferable smells.

The crime-lab people would bring more—and less— sophisticated paraphernalia: cameras, cotton swabs (for taking blood samples), fingerprinting kits, carpet knives, and sturdy axes to knock down walls.

This section of Governor Nicholls, near Jackson Square, three blocks from the river, qualified as one of the nicest in the French Quarter. At 629 a nine-foot-high brick wall guarded slave-quarter apartments (so named because pre–Civil War residents kept slaves in their homes) renting for $600-plus per month, high-dollar pads in 1980.

Inside double wrought-iron gates opening into a courtyard adorned with a bubbling three-tiered fountain stood two uniforms, men I knew, Mike Nieves and Tim Brown.

"What've you got?" I asked.

"White male, age fifty-seven," Nieves said. "Cut to ribbons."

"Where?"

"Lower apartment. The one under the steps."

Fred went inside. I talked to Nieves and Brown.

"We received the call at one fifteen," Nieves said. "A Signal Twenty-nine." Signal 29: unclassified death. "When we arrived at one eighteen, two subjects met us out on the street."

"Those two?" I nodded in the direction of a pair of middle-aged white men standing close together just outside the gate.

"Yes. Thomas Bloodworth, on the right, and Norbert Raacke."

"Keep them here till I can talk to them."

"Bloodworth and Raacke," Nieves continued, "were personal friends of the victim, William Hines, Jr. Hines hadn't reported to work Tuesday afternoon at the New Orleans *Times-Picayune*. Very unlike him, according to these two guys, so they came over to check. After Hewitt Law, an upstairs tenant, unlocked the gate, Bloodworth and Raacke found Hines's door ajar and stepped inside."

What they saw would stay with them always. Blood everywhere, blood on the floor and furniture, smeared on the walls and splashed on the ceiling. They saw the blood but not the body, and wisely ran to call the police.

Nieves and Brown went into the apartment, but not for

long. They found William Hines's body, slashed, almost carved up, more stab wounds than either could count. The victim lay in a nearly perfect fetal position—having left the world just as he entered it—except for one difference: he was almost decapitated.

Nieves and Brown were good cops with strong stomachs, but they wasted no time getting out of the apartment to call Homicide. And not just because they were trained to preserve the crime scene. Whoever did this was loose in New Orleans—and no one was going to feel safe till we found the killer.

Listening to the two uniforms made me wince. I wondered if perhaps Hines had surprised a burglar who then killed him. I looked up over my shoulder at the brick wall and heavy wrought-iron gates. Not likely.

Maybe a girlfriend, something snapping in her head during an argument. Or a family member. Nieves and Brown described an incredible degree of violence. Such savagery often indicated a relative, someone dear to the victim, whose emotions ran hot and deep. A burglar would stab and run.

I started into the apartment and met ashen-faced Fred Dantagnan coming out.

"Geesus, Fred," I said, glancing at him.

"It's your case. You go look."

I'd thought nothing could make Fred pale. On a murder investigation the bearlike Dantagnan resembled a machine, a robot, with the total detachment of a coroner. I don't know how he managed it, and this day he didn't.

Other homicide detectives joked about Fred, though not to his face. Seemed he always drew the bloodiest murders, but it was purely by accident, since headquarters employed a rotation system for assigning us to cases.

Fred's shaken condition startled me.

"What's it like?" I asked.

"Bad enough to gag a maggot."

I stepped into a living room Charles Manson might have ravaged. Long, bloody streaks and splatters covered each wall. It looked like the room had been sprayed with a hose, which wasn't far from the truth.

In the bedroom I saw William Hines. His throat had been slashed from ear to ear, the jugular vein severed. As he was dying, blood must have shot out with the force of a fire hose. A battle, totally one-sided, had raged throughout the apartment, with the pursuer stabbing, slashing, and the victim running, staggering—surely he screamed and screamed—dying as he searched for an escape. The smears on the walls came from his own bloody hands.

The sight both fascinated and horrified me. You'd never guess that five quarts of blood could cover this much territory. William Hines himself lay curled on the floor, caked with more dried, rust-colored blood. He had suffered multiple stab wounds of the head, neck, and upper torso. I saw numerous defensive wounds on forearms, palms, and fingers, indicating that Hines had tried to ward off a knife with his bare hands.

There was no mystery about how this murder went down. Hines, pursued, ran from his assailant, repeatedly turned to defend himself, ran again. Finally, the killer grabbed him from behind and slashed his throat.

Rigor mortis had set in. I estimated that the victim had been dead at least twenty-four hours.

Blood has its own very unpleasant smell, like iron, and I had to force myself to stay. After nine years in Homicide and several hundred murder investigations, I still had difficulty dealing with crimes like this. A certain amount of mental separation proved helpful. I thought about sailing on Lake Pontchartrain with one part of my brain while the other searched the apartment for evidence.

An open bottle of Jack Daniel's and two half-filled highball glasses sat on the kitchen table. It was possible that the killer had drunk from one of them. Good security protected these former slave quarters; the killer couldn't get through the iron gates to the courtyard without a key. Since there was no sign of forced entry, I believed William Hines knew his killer. They had drinks together. The severity of the wounds and the ferocity of the attack also pointed to a relative or friend. I thought the case wouldn't be too difficult to solve. I was wrong.

I didn't find the weapon, probably a very sharp, wide-blade knife. Unlike guns, a killer frequently leaves a knife behind. The D.A. needed that knife for tests which could tie it to the crime almost as accurately as bullets to a gun.

The apartment wasn't ransacked, further indication that William Hines hadn't surprised a burglar. Hines's wallet contained no money, but his identification and credit cards appeared undisturbed. I noticed the living room housed shelf upon shelf of books, and I could tell they'd been read, not used for decoration.

I looked around one last time at the chaos, trying to put a face on the person who caused it. Nothing human came to mind. I walked outside and joined Dantagnan to wait for the crime-lab crew.

"A fucking bloodbath," my friend said, shaking his head. "I figure the stabbing lasted a minute."

That's what I guessed. A *minute*. Each of us had survived life-threatening situations—usually gun fights—that lasted only seconds, but during the battle those seconds stretched to eternity. I couldn't imagine a whole minute.

"Hines worked for the *Times-Picayune*," I said.

"Wonderful," Fred snorted. "They'll give this a lot of coverage we sure as hell don't need."

Besides an unusually high number of murders over the past few months, an already over-extended Homicide Unit was working three or four men short. Although our jobs necessarily and primarily involved solving murders—rarely did we prevent them—we took a lot of heat from the public and the powerful *Times-Picayune.* Police brass, many of whom understood and empathized with our plight, nonetheless occasionally reacted to the criticism. In their frustration and helplessness in the face of a wave of murderous violence, the brass might bring down additional pressure on detectives already working dangerously close to their limits.

The crime lab's Timmy Seuzeneau, carrying a 35mm camera and a heavy wooden case, lurched into the courtyard. Timmy, in his early thirties, with black hair and a black mustache, resembled a young Omar Sharif. I worked with Timmy often and always found him in a good frame of mind, cheerfully willing to do unpleasant tasks, like ripping out a wall, at which others might balk.

"You guys going fishing this weekend?" Seuzeneau asked. He'd learned through the grapevine that several detectives planned a trip to Venice, Louisiana.

"Bad time to leave town," Dantagnan answered for both of us, referring to the recent spate of murders.

"Yeah." Seuzeneau agreed.

Dantagnan and I showed him through the once-tidy apartment that someone had turned into a slaughterhouse. Under our direction, Timmy used ninhydrin to dust the entire crime scene for fingerprints. He took more than fifty photographs and numerous blood samples. A minor victory for the dying Hines might analyze into a major one for us if he'd drawn blood from his attacker. Often on hands and knees, we searched the apartment with the figurative fine-tooth comb. A button torn from a shirt or a single thread from a piece of clothing could convict a killer.

Someone Hines knew—the phrase tolled in my head like a heavy bell. I needed as much background information on the victim as possible. I looked through his address book, his bank statements—maybe I could tell if he kept money in his apartment—at matchbooks he might have picked up recently while out on the town.

Veteran homicide detective Pascal Saladino had solved a murder from a phone number jotted on a book of matches. I once caught a killer by using clues from the victim's diary found a thousand miles from the crime scene. Another time, two human hairs stuck to the bottom of a rental car led me to a pair of slimebags who had killed a young bride for insurance money. And, on another case, Detective Mike Rice and I learned from friends of a victim what kind of jewelry he wore, visited pawn shops dealing in similar merchandise, and collared the murderer.

Seuzeneau fingerprinted the corpse. He even fingerprinted himself. Experience had taught him that he'd take some of his own prints from the apartment back to the lab. Timmy didn't wear gloves at the crime scene; gloves made handling evidence awkward. The highball glasses he sprayed with ninhydrin, for example, might need to be moved four or five times, and gloves can smudge a fingerprint. But an expert can lift one fingerprint off another and destroy nothing. So Timmy worked with bare hands.

Seuzeneau carefully ran a razor-sharp penknife under each fingernail of the corpse and placed the residue in evidence envelopes. Hines might have scratched the murderer; possible we could cross-match the blood in the scrapings to the killer's blood. If we ever caught him.

We'd worked the crime scene about an hour when Dr. Franklin Minyard arrived. This brilliant, kindly man, truly one of the city's most valuable assets and a world-renowned coroner, earned the nickname "Dr. Jazz" in New Orleans because of his outstanding trumpet playing. On many occasions I'd heard him perform with Pete Fountain and Al Hirt, and several times he'd lent incalculable assistance on homicides I was handling. However, he seldom showed up at murder scenes.

"What are *you* doing here, Doc?" I asked.

"I live in the neighborhood," he said.

Okay. But although Dr. Minyard had come simply as a good neighbor showing concern for what happened in his own bailiwick, I sensed an unvoiced urgency. I knew this case would generate serious trouble if not solved quickly. Murders happened somewhere else, in the Desire or Florida projects, not in this patch of comfort and sanity surrounded by—but no longer safe from—the madness of the French Quarter.

I've never seen a coroner wear anything but a poker face around a corpse, and of course Dr. Minyard played the part perfectly. He always exuded monumental detachment and possessed an unbending commitment to truth, even in cases where political expediency might tempt otherwise. A totally objective man. I felt I could bet my life on what he told me.

Minyard calmly joined the surreal setting: Seuzeneau, Fred, and I resembling hunched-over ghouls, moving from blood stain to blood spatter to blood puddle. The fine silver fingerprinting dust gleaming everywhere lent an additional sense of eeriness. The carpet was cut up, drawers were pulled out, closets emptied, and cushions overturned—now the apartment did look ransacked.

But Minyard had seen much worse. Sometimes we had to go under the flooring and tear out plumbing in search of evidence flushed into pipes. If the property owner submitted a claim to the government, officials would send out city carpenters, plumbers, and other workmen to repair the damage.

Minyard told the truth about his unusual presence at a crime scene; area residents treasure these historical homes and so does the city, which allows alteration only in compliance with strict building codes. Dr. Minyard, hearing about

— 17 —

the murder via Sergeant Drouant's request for a coroner's investigator, rushed directly to Governor Nicholls. I knew the "meat wagon," a beat-up old station wagon, waited outside to transport the body to the morgue.

Dr. Minyard's professional curiosity mixed with shock as he knelt next to the body. "What kind of animal," he asked, "would do this to a human being?"

He snapped on surgical gloves and probed the wounds. I knew he'd determine whether the knife had a serrated edge, if it broke off, how deep the blade had penetrated, and the type of blade.

"Look at this," Minyard said as if addressing a class of medical students. "We have multiple stab wounds on his arms, chest, and hands. Obviously some defensive, but none fatal. Look. This laceration on the left cheek. Nasty, but not fatal. Here's a good one. In the lower chest."

Minyard's expert fingers explored. "This one probably got the liver." His right hand moved up to the neck. Dantagnan edged closer. I wanted to leave. "This one did it. I can't tell if it's one long incision or multiple stab wounds, but he's cut ear to ear. Definitely fatal."

I helped the coroner's driver put the corpse in a body bag and into the wagon for the ride to the morgue for autopsy. Then Fred and I locked the apartment, and Dr. Minyard cordoned it off with the coroner's seal.

Thomas Bloodworth and Norbert Raacke waited outside the wrought-iron gates. Bloodworth seemed especially distraught by the death. The color had drained from his face, and his hands still shook. Although I regarded Bloodworth as a very important witness, thinking the murder's solution rested in Hines's personal background, I didn't consider him a suspect. Nothing pointed in his direction, and the account he had given the uniforms made sense. Moreover, his distress at merely stepping inside the apartment door was hardly the reaction of someone capable of the carnage inside.

"Mr. Bloodworth, I know you're extremely upset. But I need to ask a few questions."

"Is he really dead?" I remembered they'd seen the blood but not the body.

"I'm sorry, but he is."

"How was he killed? Shot? A robbery? What happened?"

"I can't get into the particulars. We've just started to investigate Mr. Hines's death. At this point I can only say he was stabbed."

"Who'd want to hurt Bill? He was a wonderful man. He didn't have any money. I knew something was wrong when he didn't show up for work."

"The French Quarter," said Norbert Raacke, "is getting worse and worse. There's so much crime. Evil, vicious people everywhere. No place is safe."

A prophetic remark. I tell myself I couldn't have known it at the time.

"Why can't you people do something about it?" Raacke continued. "The Quarter was a nice place once. Look at it now."

Raacke was steaming mad, but he was aiming his wrath at the wrong person. I shared his concern, would readily admit he had a point, and also wondered what could be done. But Raacke eyed me as if I were the cause.

"Why do we have a police force, anyway? Could the crime rate be any higher without you people?"

I knew it could, but I didn't want to argue. "Tell me how you fit into this," I said.

"I came with Tom to check on Bill. He was my friend, too. Now he's dead." Raacke stared at the ground, hands jammed in his pockets.

"How long had you known Mr. Hines?"

"We both knew him well," Bloodworth said. "Me for twenty years. He was my closest friend."

"I understand Mr. Hines worked for the *Times-Picayune.*"

"For twenty-two years. A brilliant man. He loved to read, and he had genuine insight into many things. He was a proof-reader at the newspaper, and no mistakes got past Bill. When he wasn't working, he spent his days reading."

"Days?"

"Yes. He worked four to midnight."

"Did he live alone?"

"Yes. He had no family here." Tears welled in Bloodworth's eyes. "I spent so much time with him. It's hard to believe he's dead." Bloodworth covered his face with his hands and turned away. William Hines had a good friend in this man. I didn't want even to think how I'd feel if something happened to Fred.

I had to persist. "Did Mr. Hines drink much?"

Bloodworth faced me, his eyes red. "I'm sorry to say, more and more over the last few years. He would get very lonely."

"Did he have any enemies? Trouble with anyone in the neighborhood?"

"Not Bill. Everybody liked Bill. He wasn't the type anyone *could* dislike. Bill didn't live a spectacular life, but he lived decently."

"When did Mr. Hines fail to report for work?"

"Tuesday. Yesterday. I came over last night after work but couldn't get through the gate. I also called. I was afraid he might be sick, a heart attack or something, because he never missed work. Today I was determined to check on him."

"When you arrived at the apartment today, did you touch or disturb anything?"

"Positively not. We saw all that blood and called the police right away." Bloodworth shook his head sadly. "It was terrible."

"Do you know who the last person was to see Mr. Hines alive?"

"No. But maybe I can find out."

"Please call me right away if you do."

I gave each man one of my cards and told them they could go home. I needed to talk with Bloodworth in much greater detail, but right now he appeared devastated, and I didn't think it necessary to prolong the ordeal.

I reemphasized the importance of finding the last person seen with the victim, the A in the ABCs of this type of homicide investigation. If the victim was last seen with a drug dealer, that fact led the investigation in one direction. If last seen with a girlfriend, it led in another.

Fred and I interviewed occupants of the five other apartments at 629 Governor Nicholls. None of them admitted giving front-gate keys to a third party, nor did anyone hear a disturbance. We didn't know when the murder took place, but no matter the hour only the very sound-asleep could have missed hearing noises. I couldn't imagine William Hines *not* screaming his lungs out as his attacker pursued him. Solid partitions inside the slave-quarter apartments and the brick wall outside made for good soundproofing, but I felt that the victim's screams could have gone unheard only in the dead of early morning. Nor did I envision a Kitty Genovese situation playing in this neighborhood: people denying knowledge because they let cries for help go unheeded.

None of the residents knew Hines well, but what they told us backed up Bloodworth. They remembered a polite, quiet man who kept to himself. One resident often saw Hines reading in the courtyard. Another recalled: "Not long ago, when I was recuperating from surgery, Mr. Hines looked in on me twice a day. He even went to the market for me and put the groceries away in my kitchen. He was a kind, considerate man, and a good neighbor."

Darkness had fallen when Fred and I finally drove to head-quarters. We passed most of the trip in silence, scenes of the hacked-up body dominating our thoughts.

I wondered if we had a maniac on the loose, if he'd kill again. Or had we encountered a one-time murderer? I didn't think so, remembering the bloody crime scene, unless the killer knew Hines well.

My shift ran from 8 A.M. to 4 P.M. and it was now after 7:00, with much work still to be done at the office. Both the extra hours on the job and the part-time security work needed to support our families kept us away from home too much, but Fred had it worse than me. Despite his ferocious de-meanor—many detectives called him "Monk," because he looked like a monk, a husky, no-nonsense cleric in charge of monastery security—I knew him as the most gentle and car-ing of family men. His seven-year-old daughter, Kelly, just the day before, asked Fred's wife, Bea: "Mommy, will Daddy visit us tonight?"

Unlike some cops, Fred didn't carouse, chase skirts, or hand over his paycheck to pari-mutuel clerks at Fair Grounds race-track. He indulged in one simple, all-consuming hobby: his family.

"It wouldn't surprise me," observed Fred as we approached headquarters, "if, when we catch this asshole, his name is Jack."

I looked at Fred, a man not given to exaggeration. He was right. Jack the Ripper could not have butchered victims much worse than what we'd seen in that Governor Nicholls slave-quarter apartment.

≡2≡

The murder on Governor Nicholls turned Thanksgiving into a routine workday for Fred and me. We arrived at headquarters about the same time, 7:45 A.M., for business as usual—trying to catch a killer.

It often happened this way; we'd both accepted it with our promotions to Homicide. But this instance particularly disappointed. Fred and I looked forward to a full day off: stuffing ourselves with turkey and all the trimmings, kicking back for parades and a chance to watch the Dallas Cowboys battle the Seattle Seahawks on television, and enjoying some quality playtime with our children. We specifically opted for Thanksgiving off, trading shifts with other detectives to get it, giving up Christmas Day in the process.

About noon the day before—while most civilians cleared desks for the long weekend, shelled pecans for the best batch of pralines ever, crossed fingers to make connecting flights, or prayed for good football weather—I hoped for no murder in New Orleans. I knew that with our rotation system the next homicide fell in my lap.

No one forced me to work Thanksgiving, but staying away would have been criminal. A killer filled with as much hate as the one who slaughtered William Hines had to be found quickly. Besides, my "sacrifice" didn't rank close to Fred's. This wasn't even his case.

And none of it compared with what the victim had gone through, what he lost.

I sorted through the Hines file and began briefing Fred on what I'd done and how little I'd accomplished since he went home the night before. My partner listened attentively as he puttered around the coffee maker concocting "Monk's Magic," a noxious brew undrinkable by anyone outside our coffee-logged unit.

I hoped my rundown to Fred would spark some ideas. The night before, I stayed late, stopping first at the radio room to check the computer printout of Bloodworth's call to the police. I figured we stood one chance in a million of linking him to the crime, and the printout confirmed what he told me about his reporting of the murder.

My early optimism was beginning to fade and I found myself wondering, *what to do first?* I had no physical evidence. No motive. No time of death. No suspect description to broadcast.

The killer or killers could be male, female, or both. One murderer or twenty. A transient by now safely hidden in New York City or a local I'd pass unsuspectingly on the sidewalk.

I had a body and its name.

I ran the victim's name through the National Crime Information Center (NCIC) computer for prior arrests. He had none.

Of course not, I thought. Not this bookish man who lived peaceably, never bothering anyone, never hurting a soul. His sedate life-style made the murder even more frightening.

I'd called First District, which handles the French Quarter, and asked for a record review, specifically noting anyone arrested in the last week carrying a concealed weapon. I also talked with Donald Saucier, who worked plainclothes follow-up investigations. While I covered the entire city, he was just in the Quarter, which he knew in minute detail. Saucier said he'd check around, and I knew he would.

Finally, I wrote a short report on the Hines murder, alerting other detectives to keep their eyes peeled for anything that might assist. Then I went home.

Now Fred and I sat facing each other drinking coffee at the desk we shared. The homicide room was big and gray, a cold institutional enclosure enlivened only by posters like the cynical: DON'T LIKE MY ATTITUDE? CALL 1-504-EAT-SHIT.

I shrugged my shoulders and held my palms up for Fred.

"Times you gotta make it happen," he said.

"Bloodworth's all I've got."

"Go see him. A best friend can give you all kinds of leads."

I didn't think so—not in this case—and neither did Fred.

"I'll catch First District." Fred bounced to his feet, remarkably agile for a man so strong and bulky. "I'll get that list you asked for."

He trundled out enthusiastically, making me feel bad because I felt bad. We were close. I knew he hurt from a domestic scene similar to mine.

I'd gotten home around midnight on Wednesday, and before leaving for work this morning encountered sharp words from my wife, Diane. Our Thanksgiving plans, now in shambles, had centered on our traditional family dinner at her aunt's house.

"What time do you think you'll finish today?"

"You always ask." I was peevish, taking out my problems on the main person who made them bearable. "I'm finished when I'm finished. I'll call you when I find out."

"John, I'd like to know what we're doing. What I should tell the kids. When we should come home if you don't show up at Aunt Beverly's. I never know anything."

I wondered how low I could sink. I walked over and gave her a hug, no substitute for having a husband with a work routine she could count on. "I should be able to shake free this afternoon," I said. I had no idea if this would be true. "Save me some turkey and dressing."

"I guess I'll see you when you get there," Diane said.

I glanced at my watch and wondered if 8:15 was too early to phone Bloodworth. To kill time I wandered to my mail slot for messages. The first one I saw was logged at 1 A.M. He'd already called me.

"Mr. Bloodworth," I said, holding a cup of Fred's stump water in one hand and the phone in the other, "this is Detective John Dillmann. I'm sorry to disturb you so early, but . . ."

"I'm glad you called. I tried to reach you last night. You asked me to find out who was last seen with Bill. I have that information."

"Good. I'd like to come over right away."

"All right. I live at 931 Decatur Street."

"I'm leaving now."

"Fine. I'll see you shortly."

I could have taken his information over the phone, but face-to-face interviews net better results. I can take notes without juggling the telephone in my ear, and Bloodworth might need to make calls to answer other questions: a pain in the neck if he has to hang up, call me back, hang up, et cetera. Better to sit right there with him.

In addition, the most likely way to solve this crime was to learn all I could about William Hines. Get into his head. Who could help me develop a more accurate picture of the victim and what might have led to his death than his best friend of twenty years?

I drove to Decatur Street and parked a block from the Mississippi River, across from the French Market, smack in the middle of a colorful conglomeration of shops, restaurants, and vendors.

Diane and I often walk in this area and stop for café au lait and hot beignets at the world-famous Café du Monde, the perfect place to enjoy one of her favorite tourist attractions: the tourists themselves. This part of the city has a special loveliness in the morning, with its smells of fresh fish and French bread, and its relaxed, Bohemian atmosphere.

I paused this beautiful Thanksgiving morning to take deep breaths of clear air. Paradise, in comparison to the dungeon-like sameness of the homicide room. At daybreak street sweepers lumbered through, clearing away litter and late-night hustlers now bedded down in out-of-the-way hutches. The few people up and about headed to Mass at historic St. Louis Cathedral.

Inside 931, sandwiched between an oyster bar and a gift shop, a passageway led to several apartments.

Bloodworth was still shaken. He couldn't control the coffee cup rattling in its saucer.

"I talked to the owner of a restaurant on Esplanade Avenue who saw Bill having lunch Monday with a friend."

"Do you know the friend's name?"

"John Clegg. He used to work with Bill at the *Times-Picayune.*"

"Do you know Clegg?"

"Yes. As a matter of fact, I had lunch with him the day before, on Sunday."

"Where does Clegg live?"

"In West Germany. He moved there six or seven years ago to work for Radio Free Europe. He came back on vacation last weekend."

"Where is Mr. Clegg now?"

"He's still in the States, I think. He planned to see his sister in California."

"Where did he stay in New Orleans?"

"I don't know. At a hotel, I suppose."

"Do you have an address or phone number for his sister?"

"I might. Let me check."

Bloodworth went into another room. I thought about that Monday lunch, which could have been close to the time of death. I needed the coroner's official report.

"Here they are." Bloodworth recited the address and phone number and I wrote them down.

"Does Clegg have any relatives in New Orleans?"

"None I know of. And I think I'd know."

"Mr. Bloodworth, I understand this has been very hard for you. But I want you to think carefully. Do you know anyone who wanted to hurt Mr. Hines?"

"No. No one," he said immediately.

I waited for Bloodworth to reconsider. Someone did more than *hurt* William Hines.

"I can't name a single enemy Bill had," he added.

I obtained a list, quite short, of Hines's friends in New Orleans and questioned Bloodworth closely concerning the victim's activities. Bill Hines stayed to himself, content with job, books, and the old-world charm of previously tranquil Governor Nicholls. I wasn't optimistic that those on the list would provide insight into his murder.

The morning sparkled. Knowing Fred wouldn't be back from First District yet, I took a walking tour of several hotels, trying to clear my head, purge the bloody memory. I asked if they had a John Clegg registered. Even if Clegg had remained in New Orleans, he might not be aware of the murder, though surely it had appeared in the morning papers.

On Esplanade I tapped on a restaurant window and got the

attention of a busboy busily draping tables with white linen cloths. He saw my badge through the glass, unlocked the door, and directed me to the kitchen, where I found the owner and his chef putting the finishing touches on a large pot of bouillabaisse, the soup du jour.

After introductions I asked the restaurateur, "Did you know a William Hines?"

"Yes. I couldn't believe it when Tom Bloodworth told me Bill had been murdered. That's simply horrible."

"Did you know Mr. Hines personally?"

"Yes. Well, only as a customer. But he dined at our place frequently over the years."

"Did he have lunch here on Monday?"

"Yes, with John Clegg. As I told Tom, I chatted with them a few minutes that day. I specifically remember because John hadn't been here for quite some time. Before moving to Europe he used to come in often."

"How did Mr. Hines appear to you?"

"Physically?"

"No. His mood. Was he nervous? Afraid?"

"I'd say friendly and relaxed. Parts of their conversation I heard. They talked about the newspaper and caught up on what happened since John Clegg went to Germany."

"What time did they leave the restaurant?"

"I can't say for sure. The lunch crowd had thinned out, probably one thirty or two."

"Did they leave together?"

"Yes. I said good-bye as they walked out. It's something to think Bill Hines will never come back."

Next I drove to the other side of the Quarter and called on the Bourbon Orleans, Fairmont, Place d'Armes, Bienville House, and Maison Dupuy, some of the best hotels in America.

How could I know I had visited a murder scene *before* the killing took place?

In the Maison Dupuy I grabbed a newspaper and a cup of coffee. The *Times-Picayune* ran the William Hines murder on its front page, where homicides don't often appear. This meant pressure already mounting down the line, powers-that-be wanting the killing solved quickly. But as the paper stated, "Police have few clues in the case."

I learned from the article—who would know better than his employer?—that William Hines, born in Meherrin, Virginia, graduated from Hampden-Sydney College in Virginia, and worked in the newspaper's proof room for twenty-two years.

About noon I drove back to headquarters and found it empty except for Dantagnan. His trip to First District had netted no helpful information. I thought of calling California, but decided to let it perk a little longer. West Germany and Radio Free Europe knocked around in my head, but I couldn't make any connections.

"What do you think?" I asked Fred.

"The same as you," he said. "A relative or a close friend. Or a fucking nut."

The last option was what we feared the most.

Fred and I walked the block and a half to the coroner's office, wanting to know what the autopsy showed, especially the time of death.

Assistant coroner Dr. Monroe Samuels was working this early afternoon, and we found him in the morgue. Dr. Samuels, a gray-haired man in his fifties, kindly and soft-spoken, ranked as one of the country's leading pathologists: In the field of forensic science, New Orleans takes a back seat to no city. Dr. Samuels headed the pathology department at Charity Hospital, which handles autopsies for the entire state.

Samuels padded from refrigerated box to refrigerated box,

where bodies cooled. The butcher shop smells of disinfectant, blood, and body fluids were pungent and thoroughly unpleasant. The odor didn't bother Samuels, who smoked a pipe, or my friend Fred. I had more of a problem.

Fred was pretty solid. He'd handled one case where the perpetrator had disposed of his roommate in a unique manner. "I found forty pounds of the victim," Fred always related with a straight face, "wrapped up in Reynolds aluminum foil in the freezer. The roommate had eaten the rest."

That investigation, already a legend in the department, produced the one time I saw Fred afraid. "Scariest damn confession I ever took," he recounted. "The perpetrator had crazy eyes and no remorse. He eyeballed me up and down like a piece of brisket. He wanted me for dinner."

"What can I do for you two gentlemen on this beautiful Thanksgiving?" Dr. Samuels asked.

"The dripping knife," Fred answered, figuring there couldn't have been another homicide, in such a short period, like the one on Governor Nicholls.

"The Hines case," Samuels said. "A bad one."

I'd never heard Samuels call a case "a bad one."

"What in the world happened?" Samuels asked.

His curiosity wasn't unusual. A coroner often asks detectives for details. Like any citizen, he wants to know who could commit such a crime.

"We don't know yet, Doc," I said. "We found Hines's body in his house yesterday afternoon. No forced entry. Anyone could have done it."

"This murderer's still walking the streets?" The grim Samuels stared at a spot in space. "He must have been on something to do this much damage."

I thought the same thing. If true, it meant scouring the least desirable sections of the French Quarter, trying to extract information from addicts, transients, runaways, and suspected muggers: a class of citizens who fear and despise police and honor a weird solidarity of silence, even with a maniac killer on the loose.

Dr. Samuels, slender and distinguished, led us into his small office, fished out some papers, and handed them to me.

"He sustained a total of twenty wounds." Samuels pursed his lips. "The majority not fatal." The ones I saw on his hands, arms, and face.

"Let me show you what killed him." Samuels walked around his desk and stood in front of me. He pushed his right index finger into my lower right chest. "A large stab wound here perforated the liver." He touched each side of my neck. "The carotid and jugular were severed. Either of these would have done him in for good."

"What kind of knife are we looking for?"

"Large blade. Minimum length of four to six inches."

"A kitchen knife?"

"I don't think so. The wounds are more than an inch wide. This indicates a thick blade, such as a Buck knife or a hunting knife."

This suggested the killer brought the weapon with him. Premeditation.

"It looked to me," I said, "like Hines put up quite a struggle."

"A titanic one. But once he took it in the neck, he bled out real quick."

"What about the time of death?"

The critical question. Hines had been seen at lunch with John Clegg at 1:30 P.M. on Monday.

"Maximum forty-eight hours before you found the body." That meant, at the outside, William Hines died shortly after leaving the restaurant.

"Minimum twenty-four hours before you found the body. Somewhere in that time frame."

"Geesus, Doc, can't you be more specific?"

"No. If you want a guess, and I base this on an analysis of Hines's stomach contents, I'd put it right in the middle of the twenty-four hours."

Between 1 P.M. Monday, the twenty-fourth, and 1 P.M. Tuesday, the twenty-fifth. If Samuels's guess was correct, the murder time was 1 A.M. Tuesday.

The time at which a homicide takes place can prove critical. A suspect may have time unaccounted for at one hour and be dining with the chief of police and a roomful of nuns during another.

Occasionally a coroner attempts to demonstrate more expertise than, scientifically, he can possibly possess. If, later, he stubbornly sticks to his guess, a jury may set a killer free. Samuels's inability to nail down Hines's time of death disappointed me, but I respected his refusal to showboat.

Fred and I got up to go. "I guess that's it for now," I said.

"Yeah," he said. "My job's over. Yours is just beginning." An uncomfortable smile spread across his face. "What are you guys doing out there, anyway? You need to get on the ball."

The words, coming from him, shocked me.

Fred's big head slumped. "We're trying, Doc," he mumbled. "We're trying."

We returned to the homicide room, still deserted except for Homicide Commander Steve London, on duty this Thanksgiving because a rash of murders had inundated his unit while the media growled about our not solving enough cases. A full shift of detectives worked this afternoon—out in the field, where I wanted to be—trying to solve crimes. But how, productively, should I start on such a killing?

I didn't have enough leads to occupy myself, much less Fred. "Go on home," I said, "maybe Bea kept your dinner warm."

"Why don't you knock off too? There'll be another one tomorrow. They just keep coming."

Fred didn't mean it. The sight of Hines, so many other Hineses, the holiday, and the dreary room plastered with macabre posters (KILLERS BELIEVE IN POPULATION CONTROL)— only a saint could remain optimistic. Fred was just a monk.

"I've got one phone call to make," I said. "I'll probably dig into a plate of turkey before you do."

Fred left, and I called California.

"May I speak to John Clegg, please?" I didn't know if my only murder suspect was there, but I needed to stay positive.

"He's not here right now."

"Are you Mr. Clegg's sister?"

"No, I'm not. I'm a friend of hers."

"Do you expect her soon? Do you expect Mr. Clegg?"

"I really don't know. May I ask who's calling?"

"A friend of his in New Orleans." I'd learned that if the person I called had committed murder, he'd never answer a phone message from a homicide detective.

"Oh. Wasn't John just in New Orleans?"

"Yes, but I missed him. Do you know where he is?"

"I really don't."

"It's very important I talk to him. Please tell him that. I'll give you a couple of numbers where he can reach me."

I told her my home phone number and that of Diane's aunt. I didn't leave my office number because anyone answering would start with "Homicide."

I sat at my small desk. Things had improved a little since my rookie days, when I wrestled with three detectives for space and a chance at the blower. Now only Dantagnan and I shared the desk and the single telephone.

I wondered what I could do. Drive over to the *Picayune?* No. Interviewing their holiday skeleton crew now would only lead to a follow-up trip later. I was counting a lot on Clegg, though I knew he was a weak reed to cling to.

Steve London came out of his office and headed for my desk. London, trim, dapper, alert, had risen from the ranks to his high post. When he'd been a detective, we'd worked together on several cases. Steve, blessed with a near-photographic memory, breezed through all the tests and shot up to commander.

Steve possessed the instincts of a detective. He had walked in our shoes, gone out to make dangerous arrests, and knew firsthand the problems we faced. Although he headed the Homicide Unit, London didn't view his job as merely supervisory. He was no bureaucrat. He hit the streets with his men when he thought it would help.

London, two years younger than my thirty-three, dressed impeccably in designer clothes. He never had a hair out of place, kept his shoes at a perfect shine, and was always filled with energy.

On one homicide, ulcer treatment interrupted my investigation. After checking out of the hospital early and working forty-eight hours nonstop to bring the murderer in for questioning, I looked and felt terrible. Steve took one glance at me and said, "Let me help you." He didn't have to do this, he had plenty of work of his own, but he stayed with me all day, right through the confession.

At the time of the Hines murder, London was working on his law degree; he has since become chief of detectives in St. Bernard Parish, the jurisdiction's second top law enforcement position, just under the sheriff. Steve and I share a couple of "youngest" honors: I was the youngest homicide detective in NOPD history; he, the youngest unit commander.

London, standing over my desk, energized as always, shifted back and forth on the balls of his feet like a fighter, clenching and reclenching his fists, a wry smile on his face.

"John, you're working the Hines case?"

"Right, Lieutenant."

"How do we look?"

"I need a game plan."

"No suspects at all?"

"Possibly. Hines had a friend who lives in Germany, was in town Monday, and had lunch with the victim. It may be the last time anyone saw Hines alive."

"Do I sense a trip to Germany?"

"A nice thought. But the suspect's in California, and I don't want him getting any farther away than that."

"Any motive?"

"Not yet."

"Did you find the murder weapon?"

"No."

London raised his eyebrows. He knew killers don't usually run from crime scenes carrying bloody knives. "You need any help?" He meant manpower.

"I need some physical evidence. A solid suspect."

"How come so many wounds? Your report was very graphic."

"I don't know. Drugs maybe. Or a lot of hate. Or we maybe have a hard-down nasty son of a bitch out there."

"Didn't your victim work for the *Picayune?*"

London knew he did.

"Right," I said.

"We don't need a *Times-Picayune* employee murdered," London said, seeming angry that someone had the nerve. "We're up to our asses in murders now, and they'll want this one solved yesterday." London fixed me with a stare. "How's your load, John? How many active cases?"

"Hines makes five. But I can't let Hines lie too long, or it'll end up in the bottom drawer."

The inactive murder file. A homicide like this one might

go unsolved. Often we got a lead early on—or never. So far we had nothing: no physical evidence (maybe fingerprints and blood analysis would produce leads), no witnesses, no motive, zero. If something didn't develop fast, we likely were dead.

"Well, John," London said, "I'm glad you're on this case. You can have anything you need, and I mean *anything*."

I drove to the home of Diane's aunt, Beverly Schaff, in Metairie, and sat down alone—many friends and relatives buzzing around—to eat a dinner Diane had warmed for me. My daughter, Amy, kept jumping into my lap; Todd threw a football outside in the big backyard.

Slowly my equilibrium returned. It never ceased to surprise me, the metamorphosis I underwent. I dealt with murderers day in and day out, found myself descending almost to their level, and sometimes forgot decent people made up the overwhelming majority of the population. It was a constant battle to avoid becoming a savage, and I always feared that someday I wouldn't return to normal.

Diane's mom and dad talked a lot about their favorite grandchildren, Todd and Amy. My twelve-year-old son got much better grades than his father ever achieved, and seven-year-old Amy demonstrated talent in music and painting. All credit to Diane, who often must have felt like a single parent.

Diane's father, Harold Walzer, worked for the public utility company, adored his wife, Rosemary, Diane, and Diane's sister, Linda. The Walzers were a warm, close, loving family.

Driving over Lake Pontchartrain late that night on our way home to Slidell, I caught Diane up on the Hines case. I deliberately omitted the ferocity of the killing, which I didn't think she needed to hear. As always, her sympathy immediately went out to the victim.

"What a horrible thing to have happen," she said. "And in his own home. John, I hope you catch that person soon."

"Me too," I agreed, trying to picture the killer. Every face I conjured resembled hideous mutations out of a horror flick Todd might watch.

"I think the worst is over," I said. I wanted to believe it. Perhaps three days had passed since William Hines's murder, and a roving maniac would have struck again by now.

"I think the worst is over."

My own words. They haunt me still.

3

"**H**elp! Help! Help!" screamed Rodney Robinson, age twenty-five, who lurched from Room 1095 of the posh Fairmont Hotel, staggering along the lushly carpeted hallway, blood spurting from his throat like water from a ruptured faucet, spattering walls as he went. Robinson dropped face forward onto the floor, nearly decapitated, his arms extended as if in crucifixion.

Rodney Robinson, with what friends described as a spectacular life of achievement ahead of him, died at 4:49 A.M., Friday, November 28, thirty-nine hours after the discovery of William Hines's body.

Homicide detective Mike Rice, a good friend of mine, working the graveyard shift, was contacted via police radio by Detective Martin Venezia and advised of an apparent murder at the Fairmont, located at 134 University Place. Rice proceeded immediately to the hotel and met house detective Vincent Silva.

"What happened?" Rice asked.

"Black man dead on the tenth floor."

"How?"

"Either a stabbing or a shooting."

— 39 —

Rice stared at Silva.

"I couldn't tell which," the Fairmont security man said, returning Rice's stare. "There's too much blood on the corpse."

"Who reported the murder?"

"Two guests in different rooms telephoned the switchboard to report what they believed was a homicide."

Rice rode the front elevator to the tenth floor. He first searched the hallways. The killer might not have escaped. The Fairmont, after all, had a reputation for excellent security. But Mike found the hallways deserted, and within minutes the hotel crawled with cops.

The Fairmont, the crème de la crème of New Orleans hotels, with suites costing hundreds of dollars per night, catered to important politicians and corporate moguls. The small army of police converging on the scene attested to the homicide's importance. If required to choose a site for a murder, a tourist-conscious Chamber of Commerce *might* name the Fairmont after exhausting every other place in the Crescent City.

Mike Rice, five eleven, 170 pounds, had straight dark-blond hair and a mustache. In addition to being an accomplished polygraph operator, he had earned a reputation for communicating with criminals. Mike could lower himself to their level, speak their language.

No one obtained confessions better than Mike. He listened to the recounting of a savage killing with a "this is routine, ho-hum, nothing out of the ordinary" demeanor designed to convince the perpetrator that what he did was no big deal. Misreading Rice's nonchalance, the murderer often spilled his guts to his new "friend." Rice captured the essence of the crime in the killer's own words.

Of course, Mike Rice did consider murder a big deal,

though he never let on to those he questioned. He put on an act, a necessary and effective one. Who would talk if the listener exhibited shock, horror, and outrage? The killer never knew how much he revolted Mike, at least not until he found himself serving a life sentence at Angola. Even then he probably thought others, the prosecutor, the judge, his own "incompetent" lawyer—but certainly not the sympathetic Mike Rice—had done him in.

When Mike knelt to examine the butchered Rodney Robinson, it required tremendous inner strength to muster an outward calm. Mike knew immediately that he was dealing with a savage murderer. Not a man tempted to indulge in florid prose, Rice wrote in his official report:

> Robinson was noted to be lying in a large pool of blood with a massive amount of blood about the body. On the river wall in this hallway was a blood smear leading to Room 1095.
>
> No items that could be construed as weapons of either assault or defense were noted on or about the body.
>
> The locks provided on the room's door were all found to be functional, and lacking any indication of forced entry. Detective Rice entered this room and noted a large amount of blood on the interior of the door, beginning near the chain lock and traveling downward to the floor and onto the carpet.
>
> Continuing into the room, blood was observed on all four walls and the ceiling.
>
> There was a small writing table in front of the river wall. Atop the table were several large blood droplets.
>
> On the uptown side of the room were noted two night tables, and on each table was a drinking glass containing what appeared to be bourbon.

Rice searched the blood-drenched room and found only eighty-five cents. "It is believed Robinson was the victim of a robbery," he wrote in his report.

Mike knew, the moment he spotted the savaged victim and the abattoir atmosphere, that he could expect heat and more heat from superiors demanding the perpetrator's rapid arrest. But he wouldn't catch kudos if, later, a judge declared a mistrial because Mike cut corners at the crime scene. A cool head, Rice went about his business meticulously, refusing the temptation to rush.

A shaken James and Mary Bolding of Portsmouth, Virginia, told Rice they had been sleeping in the room next to Robinson's. They heard a door slam and the sound of someone running down the hallway yelling, "Help! Help!" Neither looked out the door, but instead called the front desk. They couldn't say whether the person running was the person screaming.

Rice also interviewed Jack and Nancy Wallace from San Diego, who told of desperate shouts from the hallway awakening them.

"Describe what happened," Rice said.

"I opened my door and saw a black man lying motionless on the carpet. The poor man's face, his whole upper body, lay in a big puddle of blood. My God, what a horrible sight."

"What did you do?"

"I looked up and down the hallway, but didn't see a soul. Then I closed and locked my door and called the switchboard operator."

"When did you next open your door?"

"After the police arrived."

"How much time elapsed between your hearing the screams and opening the door?"

"Not long. Five or ten seconds."

A perpetrator can travel quite a distance in five or ten

seconds. The killer might still have been in Room 1095 when Mr. Wallace opened his door, but Rice guessed he'd fled.

Down the main elevator? Wielding or hiding a large bloody knife? Frantic? Looking—how would he look?—like a madman entering the serene Fairmont lobby? Surely he was soaked in blood. Even if the killer took the stairs, ten flights of them, he still ended up—bloody, discombobulated, and gasping for breath—in the well-secured lobby.

Rice instructed arriving detectives to conduct a room-to-room search of the entire tenth floor, and to include the complete stairwell. The case was his, just as Hines belonged to me, and the other officers unquestioningly followed his directions.

A good system. In a New Orleans homicide, one detective calls all the shots. Some cities compartmentalize an investigation, which has two disadvantages: competition between detectives leading to one withholding information from another, looking to claim credit for solving the case; or, more likely, a detective *thinking* his counterpart knows about certain evidence when in reality he doesn't, and the data going unshared.

Detective Martin Venezia, now on the scene, found a blue knit skullcap lying on the river side of the hallway, near the main elevators, 50 feet from Robinson's room. If the cap belonged to the murderer, it might convince a judge and jury to put a killer away. So Rice hoped. Instead the cap would, down the line, create a large, virtually insurmountable barrier to conviction.

At 5:50 A.M., assistant coroner Dr. Emile Riley arrived on the scene and officially pronounced Rodney Robinson dead. Preliminary examination revealed numerous signs of trauma, including cuts, lacerations, and slashes, three potentially fatal: two puncture wounds to the upper left chest—either could have pierced the heart—and one long, curved, laceration starting at the right shoulder and traversing over the shoulder into the neck.

At the Fairmont's front desk, Mike obtained a copy of Rodney Robinson's hotel registration card. Robinson occupied Room 1095 alone, arriving on November 15 and giving an estimated departure date of November 30.

Another notation caught the detective's eye: Robinson hadn't paid for the room. The Fairmont "comped" his entire stay, a "professional courtesy."

Rice learned that hotel executives considered young Rodney Robinson a sort of phenomenon in the business. Four years earlier, when only twenty-one, he worked security at the New Orleans Marriott. Distinguishing himself as a highly intelligent and industrious employee, he moved up to the personnel department. Then, in May 1978, he became assistant personnel director at the New Orleans Hilton.

Rodney Robinson's star rose higher in 1979 when he became personnel director of the newly opened Hilton Hotel in Mobile, and it continued to soar when he joined the Shamrock Hotel in Houston, also as personnel director, just three months before his murder. In 1979, Rice learned, a national restaurant chain offered Robinson a regional manager's position, but he turned it down, not wanting to live on the West Coast.

"He had an excellent future ahead," said a New Orleans Hilton employee, "and could have written his own ticket."

Rice found a parking stub attached to the registration card, indicating Robinson had use of a car in New Orleans. But a search of the Unipark Garage, which issued the stub, failed to locate the vehicle.

Mike worked with intense, deliberate speed, shuttling from the gory murder room to potentially important witnesses and back to the murder site. Night bellman Richard Landwehr, stationed on the University Place side of the hotel, said he did not see Rodney Robinson enter the hotel the previous night or during the early morning.

"Could he have come in another way?"

"Through the rear of the hotel. The Baronne Street side."

"Is that likely?"

"Most guests don't know it exists. Generally that door is used by employees. They have to pass a security guard to enter."

Or exit. Rice learned that the rear-entrance security guard, Nedra Boykin, now off duty, saw a black man run from the service elevator onto the hotel's loading dock shortly before the police arrived. The man bolted right by her, going full tilt, glancing over his shoulder several times to check for pursuit.

Rice became an instant expert on the Fairmont's inner geography. Logic and logistics made the black man, running from the hotel after using the remotely situated service elevator, a prime suspect.

Mike obtained the names of some five hundred present and former Fairmont employees, intending to compare the fingerprints of any employee ever arrested to whatever prints he found in the murder room.

Crime-lab technicians dusted the entire scene and took some fifty photos. They lifted six partials from one drinking glass, eight from another. The Do Not Disturb sign, sprayed with ninhydrin, revealed latent prints. Several more latents appeared on a notepad and the breakfast menu.

Rice double-checked everything: doorknobs, nightstands, lamps, telephone, mirrors, desktop, napkin holders, john, washbasin. He took two hair samples from the toilet and blood samples, in plentiful supply, from all over.

Later, examiners removed hair samples from the victim's body and made comparisons with those found in the bathroom. Hair identification approaches the precision of fingerprinting.

Concluding almost five tedious hours of sifting through Robinson's blood-spattered room, questioning hotel guests and employees, and supervising the collection of every possible scrap of evidence, Mike wearily secured the scene at 9:45 on Friday morning and returned to headquarters. He brought with him a record of every phone call Rodney Robinson made from his hotel room.

At headquarters Rice obtained copies of reports on all armed robberies in downtown hotels during the last six months. He suspected armed robbery as a motive because he had recovered only eighty-five cents from the scene.

One name caught Rice's eye right away: Tyrone Cole. On May 25, 1980, police officers arrested this black male at 124 University Place (the Fairmont is at 134) for attempted armed robbery, aggravated battery, and attempted murder. Cole had also been arrested on July 11, 1980, for theft and possession of stolen property; and again on October 30, 1980, at 119 University Place, for obscenity. A talk with Tyrone Cole ranked high on Rice's list of priorities.

At 11:00 that morning, not yet aware of Rodney Robinson's murder, I called my lone suspect.

"May I speak with John Clegg, please?" I assumed the woman answering was Clegg's sister.

"Hold on, please."

"Yes?" The voice sounded deep, confident.

"Mr. Clegg?"

"Speaking. Who is this?"

"John Dillmann. I'm a homicide detective with the New Orleans Police Department."

"New Orleans? I just left New Orleans. You must be the person who called yesterday. Good God! Homicide! What's wrong?"

"I need to talk to you about William Hines."

"Has something happened to Bill?"

"I'm sorry. We found Mr. Hines stabbed to death in his apartment."

"Bill? Bill's dead? No, he can't be. I just had lunch with him Monday."

I paused a moment, then added, "How long have you and Mr. Hines been friends?"

"I'm sorry. I can't accept this. Bill murdered? Is this a sick joke?"

"No. I wish I could say it is."

"I just can't believe this."

I waited for Clegg to collect himself. A detective's lot of frequently bearing bad tidings rates close to the bottom on the "Why I Want to Be a Cop" list. The worst is telling parents their child is dead.

"How long were you and Mr. Hines friends?" I repeated.

"It's incredible. Who would want to murder Bill?"

"Mr. Clegg, please. If you'll answer my questions, I'll answer yours."

"How long did I know Bill? Many years. Ten years, I'd say. We worked together at the *Times-Picayune* and kept in touch after I moved to Munich."

"You said you had lunch with Mr. Hines Monday?"

"Yes. It was a beautiful day. We walked through the French Quarter and ate at a little restaurant on Esplanade."

"Were the two of you alone?"

"Yes. I arrived the twenty-third to visit friends. Let me think . . . that night, Sunday, I had dinner with Tom Bloodworth and made a date for lunch with Bill the following day."

"What time did you finish lunch?"

"About two."

"When did you leave New Orleans?"

"Early Wednesday morning."

The day the body was discovered.

"Do you remember the flight number?"

"Yes. The eight-forty-five departure, Flight 246."

"The last time you saw Bill Hines was at lunch on Monday. Is that correct?"

"No. I saw him that night."

A break: a narrowing of the possible time of death.

"When?"

"About nine thirty."

"Where?"

"At his apartment. I borrowed his jacket that day, and a friend and I stopped by Bill's place to return it."

"Who was the friend?"

"Sidney Mazerat."

"Where does Mr. Mazerat live?"

"I don't know. I have a phone number, though."

I waited while Clegg searched his wallet and came up with the number.

"How long did you and Sidney Mazerat stay at Mr. Hines's apartment?"

"Only briefly. Perhaps ten minutes."

"Mr. Mazerat left with you?"

"That's right."

"Did Mr. Hines seem worried about anything? Was he frightened?"

"Bill was in excellent spirits. He thought things were going well for him. He had a settled, comfortable life, one that satisfied him. Not many people achieve that."

At the most, William Hines had fifteen and a half hours to live. If Samuels had guessed correctly, 210 minutes.

"I understand you're vacationing in the States."

"That's correct. Right now I'm visiting my sister. I plan to return to Munich soon."

"Where did you stay in New Orleans?"

"A small boardinghouse on Bourbon Street. Much handier than a hotel, just as good a location, and a lot less expensive."

I obtained the address of the boardinghouse and Clegg's Munich telephone number, but I didn't think I'd ever call. A guilty person wouldn't admit he returned to Hines's apartment. He wouldn't cooperate at all. Clegg reduced my list of suspects, previously numbering one, to zero.

"Well, I thank you, Mr. Clegg. If I need anything else, I'll be in touch." I didn't think this sign-off would work, and it didn't.

"Wait a minute, Detective. Who would do this? Bill had no enemies. Was he robbed? Do you know who did it?"

"Not yet. I'm still in the preliminary phase of the investigation."

"Did they break into his apartment?"

"I can't answer that question, Mr. Clegg. You need to realize this is a serious investigation. I understand your concern, but try to see my position."

My position: If I said anything, it could come back in court to haunt me. What if Sidney Mazerat were involved? Clegg likely would call Mazerat and inadvertently tip him off to what I knew, which in reality amounted to very little. But when I did learn what really happened, and so testified, John Clegg's account of what I told him now could, with the help of a good defense lawyer, cancel out the correct version I offered in court. Why should the trial jury believe me when I'd said something different to Clegg?

Citizens often judge the police overly secretive about what they know. An unfair rap. Cops employ "no comment" reactions to avoid committing themselves to "facts" that can later free a felon.

Clegg asked his last question: "Where was Bill stabbed?"

Ninety percent of the time people want to know. I've often wondered why. Why in the world?

"I'm really not at liberty to discuss it, Mr. Clegg. I thank you for your cooperation, and I'll be in touch if I need you."

I called Sidney Mazerat, made an appointment and went to see him. He corroborated everything John Clegg had said. I called on the Bourbon Street boardinghouse, and again Clegg's account checked out.

Arriving back at headquarters at 2 P.M., I was surprised to see a haggard Mike Rice at his desk. I knew he worked the graveyard shift—midnight to 8 A.M.—which put him into his sixth hour of overtime.

"What's up, Beans?" We called Mike Rice "Beans," as in beans and rice, a New Orleans tradition dating back to when wives cooked red beans all day while doing laundry—wash day was Monday, beans-and-rice day. Now it's eaten every day, and Mike is called Beans every day.

"Just what we needed," Rice said in a surly tone. "A tourist butchered at the Fairmont. You can bet your ass everybody from Steve London to the Tourist Commission will be on my back on this one."

I sympathized. As I've said, the last thing powerful New Orleanians want is murder in a top hotel. A few of these and a megabucks Super Bowl might relocate to a safer city.

But something else quickly overrode my sympathy. A cold, sick feeling came over me.

"What do you mean, butchered?" I asked.

"Just what I said. Carved up like a piece of meat. The victim was knifed in his room, over and over again. He tried to get away, getting stabbed and slashed each step of the way, and collapsed in the hallway. I tell you, John, it was sickening. Some kind of great publicity, huh?"

"How do you know he tried to get away?"

Rice glared at me. He had work to do. He'd soon have to answer a host of questions from worried brass, but he decided to humor me one more time. "Blood everywhere. Wall-to-wall, on the ceiling, for Christ's sake. Smears on the door. He ran all over trying to get the shit out of that room. Whoever killed him just kept coming."

"A wide-blade knife?"

"Yeah." Mike, already hot, looked close to an explosion.

"Was he stabbed in the throat?"

"And everyplace else."

"Tell me about the wounds."

Dead tired, Rice flared like a rocket. "Why you so damn interested, Dillmann? You want this fucking case? Here!" He shoved papers at me. "You can have it. Be my guest."

"Cool down, Mike. I'm serious about this. Tell me about the wounds." There was still a chance for a different M.O.

"All over. Chest. Back. Neck. Face. I think the one in the throat got him."

Goose bumps rose on my arms.

"What about drinks. Any drinks in the room?"

"Yeah. How did you know?"

"I think we have two victims and one perpetrator."

I told him about the Hines case. Mike nodded, knowing the chances were remote that two different killers with the identical style were running loose at the same time in the same city.

"I'd like to tag along with you awhile," I said.

The suggestion made sense. I had no clues; Rice had plenty. And he'd just received another lead. A possible informant, a Mary Maloney, had left a phone number and this message with the switchboard: "I know who killed Rodney Robinson."

≡ 4 ≡

We played for fool's mate,
the blitzlike four-move chess opening that can end a match
almost before it starts. Checkmate never results against a sophisticated opponent, but what kind of intellect did we battle? The primitive, bloody nature of the murders hardly
bespoke subtlety.

Rice and I underestimated the enemy, not physically, as a
death-dealing menace, but mentally; the killer was cunning
and shrewd.

"Mrs. Maloney," Mike said, "I understand you have information to help us solve the Robinson murder."

Neither of us any longer harbored such hope, which began
to diminish when we pulled up in front of the old, white,
cottage-size house—located on Roselawn Street in Gilmore,
a subdivision of Metairie—buffered by neatly trimmed hedges.
Hope evaporated when Mrs. Maloney, aided by a walker,
laboriously answered the door. I guessed she was in her early
eighties; loneliness was plainly written on her freshly pow-
dered, ivory-colored face. I imagined she often called news-
people, politicians, and, yes, police, anyone who'd listen.

She led us into a living room full of old furniture and family pictures. Crocheted doilies adorned the arms and back of a horsehair sofa in the uncomfortably warm room.

"I'm so happy you're here," Mrs. Maloney said. "Please, come sit in the kitchen. I have coffee ready."

What could this little old lady with blue hair possibly know about murder? What's more, I doubted if she'd ever seen the inside of the Fairmont. Next-door neighbors likely comprised her only acquaintances, plus the grocery boy, paper boy, and mailman.

My first reaction was, *Let's get out of here and solve the case; we can't waste time. Be firmly polite and leave.*

Mike and I looked at each other, deciding we could use a cup of coffee.

In the tiny kitchen, Mrs. Maloney talked about her deceased husband and showed us pictures of her great-grand-children, scattered from Maine to Wisconsin to California. I decided she had learned of the Robinson murder from Bill Elder on Channel 6; the *Times-Picayune* still busied itself making up evening-edition pages.

Mrs. Maloney served French bread with the coffee, and told us about her thirty years as a salesperson in children's wear for Maison Blanche department store. "When we ran real good sales," she said, "I always set some of the best items aside for my grandchildren." Mike, who grew up in a similar old New Orleans neighborhood, enjoyed Mrs. Maloney's reminiscences.

"I know who killed Rodney Robinson" scrawled on a message pad, an apparent lagniappe for Rice and me, had led the investigation to a detour. Unavoidable. Make the best of it, we told ourselves, enjoy this kindly old lady.

We'd have been remiss not following up the lead. This case, more than most, begged for a speedy resolution. Slogging it out searching for information from French Quarter undesirables, painstakingly piecing together Robinson's movements prior to his death, meticulous, time-consuming background checks—these methods might yet merit our pursuit. But the time bomb we imagined tensed to explode again required rapid defusing. "The first thing, and do this fast," old hand Pascal Saladino would say, "get the asshole off the street."

We talked for fifteen minutes with Mrs. Maloney. Then she put a finger to her lips, the shush sign, and spoke in a low, conspiratorial voice: "What I have to tell you, you must keep secret. I know who killed Mr. Robinson, but I need your promise, your *solemn pledge*, not to tell anyone I told."

"Yes, ma'am," Mike said. "We understand. We'll make sure no one learns the source of our information."

"I can trust your promise?" She reached over, placed a wrinkled hand on Mike's arm. "You're sure? I won't get a wink of sleep if you tell."

"You can count on us, ma'am."

"It was that Laurent boy. Things changed in the neighborhood since he moved in with his grandparents. I see him all the time through my blinds. Two o'clock. Three o'clock. Sometimes he doesn't come home till daybreak. It's shameful. Lord knows what he does at those hours."

"We'll take care of it, ma'am. We'll notify a patrol car to keep an eye on Laurent. Even if things don't seem to change, you shouldn't worry. Be assured we're watching him."

As we left, Mrs. Maloney again put her finger to her mouth. "Remember. No one can know. This is just between us. I'm so frightened here alone, now that my husband's gone. But I'm always watching. I know what goes on."

I considered myself fortunate drawing Mike Rice. We met four years earlier, after his involvement in a gunfight with a rapist at Royal and Elysian Fields. Mike, a uniform then,

came across the rape in progress—the woman held at gunpoint—and, after a running shootout through a darkened
park, captured the perpetrator. At that time Homicide handled all police-related shootings, and Martin Venezia and I
investigated.

In the following years I got to know Mike and his family well. His dad, extremely proud of Mike, delivered milk,
and his mom worked at Wembley Tie Factory. Rice's wife
Karen—her father is a burglary detective—is an extraordinar-
ily skilled critical-care nurse. They have two sons, Mike, Jr.,
and Mark.

Looking back on his 1972 rookie days in the Fifth District,
Mike said, "I was very idealistic then, and thought I could
change the course of the world."

Like most of us, he settled for something less: being a good
cop, keeping his small part of the planet somewhat safe and
livable.

Rice, a brave man, liked the action and danger of the
rowdy Fifth District—not many officers do—but couldn't resist the different, more-pressure-from-the-top challenge his
promotion to Homicide provided. Mike became much decorated, and several times, in the line of duty, found himself
perilously close to death.

"Mrs. Boykin," Mike said, "I'm Detective Rice and this
is Detective Dillmann. We're homicide investigators working
the Fairmont case. We need a few minutes of your time."

We stood at the front door of the Fairmont security guard's
Aline Street apartment, hoping, this time, to score a touch-
down on our second play. Both of us felt the potential here
for a big break.

Nedra Boykin, an attractive black woman employed by
Pendleton Security Services, worked the Fairmont's graveyard shift. Wrapped in a pink chenille housecoat and fuzzy

slippers, she now blinked at us sleepily. We'd awakened her at 2:30 P.M. this Friday, November 28.

"Come on in," Nedra Boykin said. "You have to excuse the apartment. My husband works days, and I work nights. It's hard to keep the place straight."

She led us into the living room, seated us on a large, soft sofa, and lit a cigarette.

"Nedra," Mike said, using her first name. Although not a police officer, she worked in a related field, with a similar goal, making informality okay. "How long have you been assigned to the Fairmont?"

"A little over a year."

"Do you always work graveyard?"

"I have so far. I sit in the guardhouse by the rear service elevator, which opens onto the loading dock."

"When did you see this subject?"

"He came running out of the service elevator and slammed head-on into the guardhouse."

"Ran into the guardhouse?"

"Yeah. Pow! Sounded like an explosion. Scared the shit out of me."

"What time did this happen?"

"Five A.M. I looked at my watch."

Robinson died about 4:49 A.M., the time the hotel switch-board logged the two calls from the guests.

"Did you get a good enough look at him to give us a description?"

"I think so. It happened very fast. The bell on the service elevator rang, and I thought someone was coming down to put out trash. When the doors open, suddenly this dude flies out and runs smack into my guardhouse. A black man, about five nine, a hundred fifty to a hundred seventy pounds. In his late twenties, with his hair in a short Afro. He wore blue jeans and a blue jacket."

"I take it he banged that guardhouse pretty good."

"*Real* hard. It knocked him back. But he recovered quick, and was a gone pecan. Man, he took off. Jumped the steps and ran down the alley toward University Place."

The alley parallel to the Fairmont.

"Was he armed?"

"Possibly. He kept his right hand in his jacket pocket."

"Did you chase him?"

"No. I couldn't have caught him if I'd wanted to, and I didn't try. I had no idea what he'd done. Understand, I don't carry a gun. Besides, the way he ran, I thought someone was chasing *him*."

"Had you ever seen this man in the hotel? Could he be an employee?"

"It's possible. I don't see many employees where I sit. They know I'm there, and my job is chiefly to guard against internal theft."

"Did you notice any blood on his clothes?" Robinson's killer would have been soaked.

"I didn't see any blood, but I wasn't really looking for it."

"When did you learn one of the hotel guests had been murdered?"

"Shortly after five. When I heard all the sirens, I radioed hotel security, and they told me."

"Nedra," I said, "why didn't you give us this information this morning? The individual coming off that elevator could be the perpetrator."

"I did give it. I told the hotel security personnel, and also one of the uniformed officers. I waited around to talk to the detectives, but by seven A.M. I had to get my kids off to school. It's hard, you know, when you and your husband work different shifts."

The killer could have entered and exited the Fairmont from either the front or the back. He hadn't gone *in* at the rear, or Nedra would have seen him. If he entered by the front, he passed the concierge station, the front desk, and security guard Richard Landwehr. Yet no one noticed him. In that hotel, they *would* have noticed those blue jeans.

Equally perplexing, when did Rodney Robinson come in? Did he walk in with his killer? Probably. But they might have made their entrance during a different shift. We needed to check, and we had to establish Robinson's whereabouts in the hours preceding his death.

So far we'd found nobody at the Fairmont except Nedra Boykin who might have caught a glimpse of the killer. If she hadn't, we faced a huge coincidence: a suspicious person fleeing the hotel shortly after a brutal murder. I started to have a little hope.

"Am I the only one who saw this dude?" Nedra asked.

"Looks that way right now," Rice said.

"Will they call me to testify? I have three children."

"Whoa, hold on, Nedra; you're racing too far ahead. Any testimony is a long way down the road yet. First we'll show you some pictures to ID when we have a suspect." Rice didn't say, "Right away, as soon as we can set it up," both of us thinking about Tyrone Cole. "You don't have any problems with that, do you?"

"No. I'll be glad to help. As a matter of fact, once I tried to join the police force myself. I just don't want my name in the newspaper, that's all."

We left Nedra Boykin's apartment, turning our attention to Tyrone Cole, he of the three arrests—from obscenity to attempted murder—all in very close proximity to the Fairmont.

It was 3 P.M. and Rice had been on duty since midnight. "Beans," I said, "you better go catch some Zs. Your eyelids look droopy."

"I could use some sleep, but let's see what's happening," he replied with a slight smile.

"Our first priority is Cole. He could be our man."

"Maybe. But we can't have him arrested just because he's been popped three times around the Fairmont," he said ruefully.

"It gives us probable cause to pick him up," I countered. "We have a process of elimination here. But let's get a mug shot of him and take it to Nedra. Fred and I can handle that. If Nedra does ID Cole, you and I can bring him in at midnight."

"Sounds good. But if you get the ID, call me and I'll come in early. Call me either way."

Mike dropped me at headquarters and drove home. I went upstairs and entered Cole's name in the NCIC computer.

We'd have been negligent not to zero in on Tyrone Cole. In May of that year, he attempted to rob a tourist at gunpoint, only thirty feet from the Fairmont's front entrance. The tourist didn't produce his money fast enough, and Cole shot him in the abdomen. Uniforms apprehended Cole, charging him with attempted armed robbery, aggravated battery, and attempted murder.

Why wasn't Tyrone Cole in jail?

I suspected that the victim recovered, went back to Ohio, or wherever he lived, and refused to return to New Orleans to prosecute. It happens often, unfortunately. Many citizens, even those shot in the stomach, don't want to be bothered, and allow criminals to resume the prowl.

While out on bond in July, Cole got nabbed snatching a purse from an unsuspecting pedestrian, again in the 100 block of University Place. The judge set bail for this offense, and Cole currently awaited trial.

You'd think, with his record, he'd walk the straight and narrow before appearing in court. Not Cole. In October—last month—a uniform arrested him for obscenity (exposing his person), again in the 100 block of University.

Why his infatuation with the 100 block of University Place? Perhaps, like Willie Sutton when asked why he robbed banks, Cole would've said, "That's where the money is." Wealthy people loaded with cash and jewelry can always be found near the Fairmont. A felon can make off with more loot in one robbery there than from a dozen somewhere else.

With *three* felony arrests, why did Cole remain out on bond? Again, I believed that the individual who brought the obscenity charge had refused to press it. The computer didn't say. I merely guessed.

The obscenity charge stood as an anomaly. The Willie Sutton theory explained Cole's armed robbery and purse snatching. But obscenity? The first two crimes indicated violence; obscenity made little sense linked to that M.O. I wondered if Cole could be unbalanced enough to commit the two bloody murders we were investigating.

The computer description of Cole closely matched what Nedra Boykin gave me and Rice: black male, medium height and build, late twenties. We might wrap up the two cases tonight. Cole certainly fit a violent enough profile.

I went to the second floor of police headquarters carrying Cole's Bureau of Identification number and secured a color mug shot of the suspect: front and side views. I studied the photo closely, then leafed through hundreds of others to find five people who closely resembled him.

Whenever a prosecutor offers into evidence a photo-lineup ID, the defense considers it standard operating procedure to challenge its validity, usually at a preliminary hearing during a motion to suppress evidence. The defense attorney attempts to convince the judge that the lineup process was tainted, claiming his client's photo for some reason "stood out" or the officer coerced the witness into identifying the picture.

A black male suspect, twenty-five years old, with a mustache, should be grouped with photos of similar-looking men. If the suspect has light skin, you don't choose pictures of people with dark skin.

The detective needs to walk a thin line. I didn't want sextuplets, making an identification impossible. Conducting a photo lineup that withstands a judge's scrutiny requires fairness, common sense, and experience.

I arrived back at Nedra Boykin's apartment at six. Her three children, aged sixteen, fourteen, and eleven, and her husband were home. Henry Boykin worked as a supervisor with the Sewage and Water Board. I apologized for coming during the dinner hour—the delectable smell of roast beef filled the house—and explained what I needed. The kids and husband crowded close as I laid the six photos on the table in two rows of three.

"Nedra," I said, "please, take your time and look at these photos closely. Tell me if you recognize anyone."

I had to use this procedure. If I said, "One of these men possibly killed Rodney Robinson," a court would rule the lineup inadmissible. The judge would hold that I exerted undue pressure on the witness to identify a murderer by implying, "Pick him out." If I conducted the lineup improperly, subsequent steps—arrest, interrogation, *confession*—might never reach the jury's ears as testimony.

So far a judge had never thrown out any of my photo lineups, but I had seen several murderers walk on other cases for precisely that reason. In one case, a gun, the murder weapon, was ruled inadmissible because the search which uncovered it stemmed from an illegal photo identification.

"Can I handle them?" Nedra asked.

"Okay," I said. "But only look at the pictures. Don't turn them over."

Often the individual's mug shot has his name on the back.

If the witness recognized a name—Cole's, for instance, because of his three arrests in the area—the lineup could be inadmissible. This sounds far out, but it happens, and a homicide detective needs to exercise extreme care: Let's say Nedra's friend, who works in Homicide, heard Rice or me mention the name Cole, and relayed the information to her; Nedra might think she was doing us a favor by fingering him. I've seen just such a scenario unfold.

Nedra picked up the pictures one at a time and held them close to her face. Then she studied them as a whole. I waited, watching her reaction to each photograph.

Finally she shook her head. "I can't really tell from these pictures. I'd have to see him in person. He ran so fast, I got a better look at his build than his face."

"You've never seen any of these people before?"

"I can't say I did. I can't say I didn't. These pictures only show shoulders and faces. I have to see the whole body."

"No problem. Let me ask you one more thing, Nedra. I realize you only saw him for a few moments, on the dead run, but you indicated to Detective Rice and me that you thought you could make a positive identification. Do you still feel you'll recognize him if you see him again?"

"In person, I think so. But not from a picture."

I doubted she'd succeed. The suspect appeared suddenly, running, and fled in the 5 A.M. darkness down an alleyway. Dress up *anyone* in a scene reenactment, and Nedra might ID him. A defense attorney would have a field day with such a witness.

Nedra wanted to help—she knew the ferocious nature of Robinson's murder—but I didn't think she could. On reflection, I had several nagging doubts about her story.

Still, the coincidence of Cole's three arrests, two of them violent, in the Fairmont's immediate vicinity, made him our prime suspect. Nedra's confidence that she could identify the man running out of the service elevator minutes after the commission of the murder strengthened the need to locate and question Cole. Even if she couldn't ID him, interrogation might produce a statement, which we could analyze, investigate, and break down.

A statement starts wheels spinning. I once questioned a suspect with blood droplets on his shoes—he'd changed all his other clothing—which led to a search warrant, which led to the clothes themselves, which led to a murder conviction.

I woke up Mike Rice, as he'd requested, calling him from a pay phone, and felt foolish suggesting he go back to sleep. I said Nedra couldn't identify Cole, but that Fred and I would go hunting for him. If successful, I'd call again.

The murders of Hines and Robinson had been simple, stark, with no finesse. Maybe we'd solve them in just such a straightforward manner.

= 5 =

*P*olice in giant neon letters might as well have flashed from our unmarked car for the scores of eyes Fred and I felt watching us through the darkness. Here we were, two white guys wearing suits, in a new white car parked in the Desire Project, one of the poorest and meanest in New Orleans. Arriving on a Mardi Gras float wouldn't have made us more conspicuous.

Penetrating Desire by myself to flush out the violence-prone Tyrone Cole would be suicidal. Fred knew it. So he waited at headquarters while I conducted the photo lineup with Nedra Boykin and then rode shotgun to the project.

The perfect sidekick for this mission, Fred maintained a weightlifter's body and a cool head under pressure. Like Rice, Dantagnan enjoyed the risks of the job. He actually performed best when lives, including his own, lay on the line. Missing a dangerous arrest upset him.

At 8:30 P.M. this November 28—still the day of Rodney Robinson's murder—we would find more adventure in Desire than even Fred wanted. Low-income and federally funded, perhaps ten blocks long and twenty wide, with three-story brick buildings haphazardly scattered, it resembled a zone bombed during a World War II raid over Germany.

Broken windows, uncollected trash, and graffiti clutter the project. No grass grows here. No trees. Dogs run loose.

Several doorless bars border Desire. Hustlers, prostitutes, drug users, and pushers gather inside and outside these hangouts, peddling poison that creeps through the project, corrupting its innards.

Despair rules Desire. Most people in the project are decent, their only crime a lack of opportunity. But the ones in the bars live by intimidation and fear. They too have their reasons. Some think the only way to succeed is crime, and they grab the chance.

Once past the bars, we headed into the project. We encountered only the young, clustered together on every stoop. The whistling began. An effective alarm system, the whistles warned, "Police in project," and raced eerily ahead of us from building to building.

Fred and I parked in front of a concrete walkway that wound through a courtyard to buildings four and five deep off the street. The one the computer listed for Cole stood three back.

District uniforms, who might handle fifteen calls a night, often jump their cars over the curb and drive *through* the courtyard. The journey on foot, they fear from bitter experience, can invite a sniper. Of course, residents don't appreciate a squad car driving through the project's front yard. Hardly an example of good police-community relations.

Not encountering trouble in Desire is exceptional, and this night, walking to our destination, the norm prevailed. A bloodcurdling cry cut through the darkness and halted the screeching whistles. A panic-stricken woman raced out the door of a building, down five steps, and almost into my arms.

Hot on her heels came a male about the same age, perhaps twenty-eight. The man grabbed her by the hair, tearing her out of my arms, and they went thrashing to the ground in a tangle.

"Police!" Fred and I yelled. He grabbed the woman, I the man.

"The bitch cut me!" spat the man, raising his bloody hand. "The bitch cut me!" I saw blood on her face, probably from where he'd hit her.

"Police!" I said again. "Break it up!"

The man struggled mightily to loosen my hammerlock from around his neck and free the wrist I had twisted behind his back.

Fred had trouble with the woman. She hit, kicked, kneed, scratched, and gouged, trying with newfound courage to get at the guy.

Then a second female appeared, yelling and cursing at the man I restrained. "You son of a bitch! You hit my sister!" She put her fist right up to his face. "Motherfucker, don't you ever lay a hand on one of my family again!"

She jumped on the man I held, fists pounding like a jackhammer, a blur of blows. She drew blood with fingernails that tore like talons. Fred let loose the woman he held and grabbed the sister from behind. The one he freed leaped on his back, and he flipped her over his head.

Now the melee raged five ways. I clung to the guy, but the two women were Furies. In one sense, this scrap ranked commonplace to uniforms, which Fred and I once had been, but in another we faced one of the policeman's most hazardous confrontations—a domestic dispute with emotions boiling. Knowing serious injury or death often result from such struggles, especially if they last long, we had to stop the fighting and take control.

I bulldogged the male to the ground, jammed my left knee into the back of his neck—*end this quick,* my brain warned—and tried to bring his wrists together to handcuff him.

My grip kept slipping on the blood from his wounds. I cranked down the pressure with my knee to discourage resistance, and it finally worked.

In the last moments of my battle with the man, an unseemly sight, Fred fended off the women, who swatted and scratched like tigers to get at the guy. We worked as a team. Since I faced the best odds, one against one, he let my struggle run its course, figuring I'd win and rearrange our chances to two against two with the women. It's called teamwork, and we learned it on our own. The danger comes by doing it wrong once. We might never get the opportunity to practice again.

I left the male handcuffed, face down in the dirt, and stood up to deal with the women. Instead, a cacophony of sight and sound assaulted me: A crowd had formed as if by magic, thirty or forty people, and I didn't need a Ph.D. in psychology to recognize the hostility. I was taken by surprise. One moment it had been the five of us; now it was a group of sizable proportions.

But then we heard a comforting sound: the wail of sirens in the distance. Someone, bless that person's heart, had called the police.

Just last a minute or two, I told myself and stood next to Fred, jousting with the sisters, trying to keep them off us and the disabled man on the ground. We didn't dare use sufficient force to subdue the women, not knowing how the crowd would react. So we pushed and shoved, saying "Police!" and "Cool it!" a dozen times. But the women were buoyed by the crowd now openly urging them on, an ugly, scary situation, each succeeding charge more determined than the last.

Then the bombshell dropped.

"He's got a gun!" a voice shouted from the crowd.

Forty people scattered in forty directions, vanishing as suddenly as they'd appeared. Only one remained, and I saw the gun in his hand. Fred and I reflexively drew our weapons—his a .38-calibre snub-nose, mine a .357 Magnum—the moment we heard the warning.

"He's got a gun": the four most frightening words in the project. The sisters froze momentarily, then they too split, running scared in separate directions.

The man on the ground yelled, "Hey, that's my brother! Don't shoot him!"

We didn't want to. He held the gun, a .22-calibre Saturday night special, at his side, but if he raised it we'd have to fire. Both Fred and I had our guns leveled down on him.

He decided to run, not the best choice, but better than shooting at us. He executed a crossover step and scrambled through the courtyard toward one of the brick buildings. Fred took off after him, yelling "Halt! Police!"

I saw the two of them, separated by thirty feet, head into the building and up a dark stairwell. At any moment I expected to hear gunfire.

I felt afraid for the first time since the incident began. This could go bad quick. And Fred was alone with the gunman.

The silent courtyard lay as deserted as when we entered it: only two people in the ghetto stillness, myself and the hand-cuffed man on the ground. I retrieved my hand-held radio, which had fallen to the walkway during the scuffle, and said into it, "Ten twenty-eight"—a police code to clear the channel for an emergency message.

"Go ahead, Ten twenty-eight," monotoned a dispatcher's steady voice.

My own didn't sound so calm, with the life of my best friend in danger. I forced myself to get the words right. "This is unit thirty-one forty-two. I'm in the four-thousand block of Louisa Street. My partner chased an armed suspect into a building across the courtyard from my position. I repeat, the suspect is armed."

Three different units came over the air almost simultaneously.

"I'm a block away."

"Give me a description."

"Ten ninety-seven."

The middle response made no sense to me. A *description?* But the last response (1097: unit on the scene) rang like sweet music in my ears. Undoubtedly the siren I heard earlier. Then the squad car, crunching over the curb and straddling the walkway, came right at me. Two uniforms sprang out of the vehicle before it fully stopped. I directed one of them to the man on the ground and raced with the second toward the building. "Be careful," I said to the uniform as we ran. "My partner's up there."

I didn't want him shooting Fred.

Before we reached our destination I saw a second unit, blue lights flashing, jumping the curb and heading up the walkway. I knew other cars would soon arrive. When more than enough had reached the scene, someone would Code Four, meaning no other units should respond. I hadn't issued a 108, officer in trouble, because no shots had been fired. If they had, or if we'd found ourselves getting our asses kicked in that fight, I'd have done it.

I used 108 sparingly. Whenever it went over the air, police seemed to trample one another in their haste to respond. When a 108, a brother in danger, gets issued, every cop within a reasonable distance—and some farther away—stops what he's doing and hurries to the scene. I know of officers who, in violation of departmental policy, rolled on a 108 with prisoners in the backseat of their unit. Cops leave a racetrack, pari-mutuel ticket in hand, horses thundering down the stretch, and even the warmth of a bed and a beautiful wife or girlfriend, to answer a 108. Detectives come, undercover people, officers off duty, individuals in tennis duds or fishing attire—however they're dressed, they come when a cop needs help.

The most important reason to use caution exercising a 108 is the danger to the public and police. The cops drive fast on their way to assist, very fast. They can get hurt, and so can bystanders.

The uniform and I stopped when we reached the front door leading to the dark stairway. "Fred!" I called out. "Where are you? Are you all right?"

"Top floor. Apartment C. Come on up."

We climbed to the third floor and found Fred, gun held up near his ear, standing back against the wall next to a steel apartment door. He did this from habit, a good one. A .22 slug wouldn't go through that door, but plenty of other bullets would.

"He's in here," Fred said. "The door slammed when I hit the second level. This is the only one it could be."

"He still got the gun?" the uniform asked.

"Yeah. I think so. I didn't see him drop it."

We heard voices from the first floor. More cops. They yelled, "What do you have? Where are you?" and I called back, "Armed subject locked in apartment. Third floor. Somebody cover the rear."

The third floor, like the entire inside of the building, lay in pitch darkness. Light bulbs in hallways, landings, and stairwells disappear quickly. People steal them—even a light bulb is a major expenditure for some—or criminals remove them: Their business is best conducted in the dark.

Flashlights provided what illumination we had. Fred beat his big fist on the door. "Police! Open up!"

We heard noises inside, but no answer. Every twenty seconds or so Fred's first hammered the door. "Police! Open up!"

Had the door been a flimsy one, we might have kicked it in, but we needed a sledgehammer (used in dope raids) to knock this one down.

"Police! Open up!"

Geesus, I thought, *make it easy on yourself.* Other methods, much more unpleasant, soon would become necessary. Right now, at worst, he faced a carrying-a-dangerous-weapon charge, which would go harder on him if he were a convicted felon. Then he might be looking at five years.

"Police! Open up!"

Even for a convicted felon, it wasn't worth a confrontation he couldn't win and which might cost his life.

"Okay," came a voice from inside. "I'm comin', I'm comin'."

We, five of us now, heard several locks unlatch. All of us seemed to be talking.

"Come on out."

"Keep your hands where we can see them."

"Put your hands on your head."

"Come out slow, asshole. Let's see your hands."

"Slow. Real slow."

The door opened two inches, four, six. He took one step, empty hands held straight out, and four of us grabbed him at once. Speed, lightninglike surprise, is always a good weapon. Even one-on-one, quickness and decisiveness overcome size almost every time.

We slammed him against the wall instantly, and the handcuffs went on a second later. It was all over.

The uniforms took him downstairs. Fred and I searched his apartment, found the gun, and gave it to an officer outside. A car whisked the subject to Central Lockup for booking, and he turned out to be a convicted felon (burglary—that's why he ran). Still, he definitely made the right choice, dealing with us instead of the SWAT team.

The flashing blue lights disappeared. In all, eight units responded before others got called off. At last, Fred and I, dirty from the fight, stood once again in the courtyard. Residents milled about. When the small army of police had shown up, they had come back out, knowing it was safe.

Having seen the body of William Hines, and having read in grisly detail about Rodney Robinson, I hadn't thought anything could get my mind off the purpose of this trip, but for just a moment Fred and I stood mute in the courtyard.

"Let's go ahead, okay?" I said.

"Cole."

"He's why we came here."

Tyrone Cole. The Hines murder scene flashed in my mind. If Cole had been the killer, the subject with the .22 we had rousted out ranked as a piece of cake compared to what awaited.

The apartment stood on the first floor. I knocked as I might at a friend's home. I didn't want to alarm him. I wanted to talk to him.

"Who's there?" A woman's voice, with a real tremor of fear.

"Police officers," I said in a nonthreatening, nondemanding tone. "We'd like to talk to you."

"Police officers. Oh, Lord, I'm coming." We heard her unlatch *five* bolts. Perhaps forty-five, short and thin, she was neatly but inexpensively dressed, her hair tied back in a graying bun.

"Is this the Cole residence?" I said.

"Yes. What's wrong?"

"We're looking for Tyrone. Is he home?"

"What did that boy do wrong? I told him over and over about hanging on those streets. What has he done now, mister?"

"Nothing, Mrs. Cole. We just want to talk to him."

"He doesn't stay here. I haven't seen him since he got out of jail a couple of weeks ago. Mister, isn't there something you can do with him? Can't you keep him in jail? I feel just helpless. He's in trouble all the time. He won't stay home, and there's nothing on those streets but trouble. What can I do? I'm trying to raise six children in this project. None of them give me problems. Only Tyrone. He's a good boy, but I fear what's going to happen to him. I fear what will happen to me. He's so crazy, I'm afraid he might hurt me."

"Does Tyrone live in the project?"

"In St. Thomas. I hear he's been staying with some girl since he got out of jail."

"Where in St. Thomas?"

"I don't know. He only calls me when he needs something."

"What is the girl's name?"

"Alicia. Alicia Pearson. All I know is her mama works at Charity Hospital."

"Does Tyrone work?"

"Work? That boy ain't worked a day in his life. That's why he's in trouble all the time. He steals. I didn't raise him that way, mister. This is a good Christian home."

"Do you have a phone number where we can reach him?"

"No. But I think he has to appear in court."

I left my card with Mrs. Cole, asking her to contact me if she learned her son's address. She asked one more time if Tyrone had gotten in trouble, and I said no. I doubted I was telling the truth, but what could I say? No stronger love exists than a mother's for her child, and I didn't want to alarm her more than I'd already done by showing up.

* * *

Back at headquarters, just before 11 P.M., we took a first good look at ourselves. My face had dirt smudges, and the knees of my pants were soiled. Fred had a rip in the seam of his jacket, a casualty inflicted by the second sister leaping on his back.

Mike Rice, starting graveyard early, couldn't resist. "Can't take Fred anywhere, can you?" Rice said, looking us over, a malicious gleam in his eyes, sizing up that we'd been in a fight. "You look this bad, what's the other guy look like?"

"How you know it was a guy?" Fred asked.

"Piss on you, Dantagnan."

Cops come up with clever lines like this.

We decided to withhold the fight information from the macho Mike. I caught him up on our search for Cole, and he said he'd pick it up right away. Utterly drained, I went home to Diane.

≡ 6 ≡

I started the new shift the way I ended the previous one: talking to Mike Rice. Before I had a first swallow of coffee, I saw him headed my way with an arrest register in hand.

"Any luck with Cole, Mike?"

"None. You'd hardly left the office when we caught a police shooting."

When an officer becomes embroiled in a gunfight, regulations automatically shift everything else to the back burner for those on Homicide watch. Even Cole had to wait.

"Who?"

"A kid in the Fifth. Bentley. Two years on the job. You know him?"

"No. Is he all right?"

"Yeah. A one oh three." Family disturbance. "It turned into a hostage situation with a three-hour standoff. They couldn't get the husband out. Finally, when he started beating on his kids, Bentley and his partner went in. The asshole fired a couple of shots, then caught one in the gut."

"Bentley and his partner okay?"

"Just shook up. The wounded man's at Charity in stable condition. He'll be okay."

"Who popped him?"

"Don't know yet. Bentley fired once, his partner twice. The crime lab's running tests now, but I'll bet Bentley got him."

"Sounds cut and dried."

"It was. But we had to take statements from the wife, two kids, three neighbors, and a shitpile of police. I've got more statements to get tonight."

"Do you need anything?"

"Yeah. For you to look at this." He handed me the arrest register he carried.

My eye opened without that shot of coffee. Officer Susan Graham, working a paid detail at the Marriott Hotel, 500 Canal Street, at 3:45 this morning, Saturday, November 29, collared a Tanya Bradford for theft, carrying a concealed weapon, and resisting arrest. The weapon: a twelve-inch butcher knife.

A friend at Central Lockup, knowing about the Robinson murder, called Mike when authorities booked Tanya Bradford. Mike went to the adjoining building on South White Street and picked up the register. "We need to talk to Graham," he said to me.

A woman could have killed Robinson and Hines. A Mr. Goodbar—the case where a woman in a singles bar invited her killer to her apartment—with the sexes of the victim and murderer reversed. The Fairmont homicide occurred very early in the morning, and neither the apartment nor hotel room had a forced entry, indicating the victims asked the killer inside. Robbery might be the motive, and Bradford, arrested at 3:45 A.M. in a French Quarter hotel with a knife, had been charged with theft. Rice was right. We should talk to Graham.

We found her patrolling St. Charles Avenue, where the streetcars still ran. She and her partner, just off a disturbance call at one of the many bars on tree-shaded St. Charles, welcomed our offer to buy them coffee. We settled into a twenty-four-hour restaurant on the corner of Jackson.

Officer Graham, five feet six inches tall, twenty-five at the time, an attractive, single woman with auburn hair, always projected energy and enthusiasm. Well liked in a job dominated by macho males, she worked the turbulent Sixth District—the "Bloody Sixth"—which includes the Magnolia and St. Thomas projects. Susan later became a burglary detective, earned promotion to sergeant in 1985, and currently investigates alleged police corruption through the Special Integrity Unit.

"Susan," Rice said, "we heard you had trouble with an arrest on your Marriott detail this morning."

"Yeah. How did you find out?"

"That's why we're detectives and you're not." He laughed, saving the day. "Seriously, Susan, what happened?"

"It started as a routine arrest of a black hooker for ripping off her date. But when I began to frisk her in the hotel security office, the bitch tried to orchestrate me."

In other words, Bradford said okay to the search, then proceeded to tell Graham *how* to conduct it—"I'll stand here, you stand there," etc.

"I became suspicious right away," Graham continued. "I put her up against the wall, and she came off like a tiger. It took a minute or two to cuff her. You're not going to believe this, Mike, but the woman had a butcher knife concealed in her boot. I'm convinced she meant to stab me. She tried her damnedest to turn the tables and put me in a vulnerable position. She wanted to get to that blade something bad."

"You okay?"

"Fine. But you haven't heard the best part. Bradford rips

off her date, a hotel guest, for eight hundred bucks. He makes a beef to the house dicks. Unusual in itself, a trick making a beef, right? Well, I catch her sneaking out the hotel and recover the john's money. When I return it to him, he counts the eight hundred dollars and tries to give me back a hundred. This guy's very sincere about everything. He tells me to reimburse the hooker, that she's earned it. 'I always pay my bills,' he said."

"The last honest man," Rice said sarcastically.

"Or something," Graham said.

"Is the hooker local?" I asked.

"Yeah. She works Decatur Street and a few hotels on Canal. A regular. Central Lockup needs a revolving door for offenders like her."

"She work the Fairmont?"

"She could."

Tanya Bradford's 3:45 A.M. arrest occurred in the same predawn time period as Rodney Robinson's murder twenty-three hours earlier. How many people are out at that hour? The scene, the time, the weapon all fitted. The john only complained because Tanya got greedy and took more than their agreed price. He didn't realize she had ripped him off until after she left. Perhaps Hines and Robinson caught her robbing their wallets. In addition, Hines's Governor Nicholls address is only two blocks off Decatur Street, Tanya's home base, and the Fairmont's only five blocks from the Marriott, where she got arrested.

Coincidences stacked on coincidences. Graham, no alarmist, described an extremely violent individual who, she was convinced, "meant to stab me."

Most hookers hook because they're hooked. Drugs create insatiable appetites only major money can feed. So much crime, often violent crime, is drug-related: more than *fifty percent.* Users do anything to quell their need, a ravenous hunger that can turn an addict into a vicious, crazed killer.

A macabre thought raised its ugly head: If the Marriott john, who wanted Susan Graham to give the hooker $100 for services rendered, had earlier caught Tanya Bradford rifling through his wallet, he might have screamed about losing more than money as he staggered along a corridor, nearly decapitated.

"Susan," I asked, "did anyone see Tanya come in with the john?"

"Yes."

And they would have said nothing. The Marriott, not an inexpensive hotel, won't tell a $1,000-a-week guest whom he can invite to his room. A different story if Tanya entered the hotel lobby unescorted. The Marriott's in-house security forces quickly show the door to prostitutes, vagrants, and street hustlers.

Interesting that Tanya had been spotted accompanying the john into the Marriott, but Fairmont security, equally adequate, saw neither Rodney Robinson nor his killer.

"You said Tanya carried a knife twelve inches long. Did it have a wide blade?"

"Yes. About an inch and a quarter. An Old Hickory, I think."

"Where's the knife now?"

"The property and evidence room."

I looked at Mike and we got up to go.

"You're handling the Fairmont murder?" Susan asked.

"Mike is."

"Why are you along?"

I shrugged.

A citizen—a Thomas Bloodworth or a John Clegg—asks only a fraction of the questions an interrogated police officer does. As we edged away from the table, I braced myself for a flurry of whys and hows from Susan Graham.

"Do you think Tanya's involved?"

"Could be," Rice said.

"The Fairmont victim was stabbed, right?"

"Yeah."

"Was he robbed?"

"Don't know."

"Had he been with a hooker?"

"Don't know."

"And that's why you're detectives and I'm not?"

"Give me a break, Susan."

"It occurred early in the morning, right?"

"Yeah."

"Will you let me know if it's her?"

"Positively."

"Will you—"

But Mike and I were at the door and gone.

We had Tanya Bradford brought from a holding cell to one of the small interrogation rooms at Central Lockup. A female correctional officer led her into the six-by-eight gray steel room with its small desk and two chairs. Rice sat behind the desk, and I stood beside Tanya.

She was five six and dark skinned, weighing a hundred and thirty pounds. The loose-fitting jail-issue jumpsuit didn't hide her full, shapely figure. Perhaps twenty-two years old, with close-cropped hair, she was naturally attractive without the makeup, jewelry, or wig she wore to work the streets. She had the large inquisitive eyes and fresh complexion of a college coed, but Tanya didn't go to school.

Did she commit murder?

The possibility existed. Tanya's arrest in a high-class hotel so close in time to Robinson's murder, with a wide-blade knife hidden in her boot, made her a mandatory interview. Still, it bothered me that another "something" kept us from going after Tyrone Cole.

Rice asked the questions. As I've said, he's good at it, a chameleon, able to go up or down to any level from a bank president's to a homeless person's.

"Tanya," he said, "have a seat. My name is Detective Rice and this is Detective Dillmann. We want to talk with you."

"Detectives? I thought you were my attorneys. Don't I get an attorney? I've already spent eight hours in this dump. What time will the magistrate set my bond?"

She had first-hand knowledge of criminal justice procedure in New Orleans.

"Tanya, how many charges do you face?"

"Three, I think. All of them bullshit. I just want to make my bond and get out of here. My lawyer will take care of this."

"Twelve-inch butcher knife. That's a pretty serious charge, Tanya."

"Not mine. They put that knife on me."

"They who?"

"Those stinking hotel cops. They don't like me coming in their hotel. They'll do anything to keep me out."

If she confessed to what happened in the Marriott, we couldn't use the information, and Rice knew it. She hadn't been read her rights. The truth is, we didn't care a whole lot about her and that john. Murder concerned us; and before the mention of murder, Rice would recite *Miranda*. I suspected the moment was at hand.

"How long you been a working girl?"

"Why the hell do you care? What do you two want, anyway? Huh! Detectives!"

"Tanya, before we go on, I need to advise you of your rights."

"Rights? Baby, I know my rights better than you do."

"You're a suspect in a murder we're investigating. You—"

"Murder! Wait a damn minute! I don't know anything about a murder." The cool facade came down. Confident of her chances against charges from the Marriott, homicide was a totally different shooting match.

"Tanya," I said, "just listen to what Detective Rice has to tell you."

"I want to review your rights," Mike said. "One, you need not make any statements: that is, you have a right to remain silent. Two, anything you say may be used against you in trial. Three, you have a right to consult with and obtain the advice of an attorney before answering any questions. Four, if you cannot afford an attorney, the court will appoint one to represent and advise you. Five, you have a right to have your attorney or an appointed attorney present at the time of any questioning or the giving of any statement. Now, do you understand what I've said to you?"

"Sure I understand. But I don't know anything about a murder."

"Then you won't mind answering a few questions."

"To get a murder rap off my back I'll answer anything. I don't need this shit. My old man will be real pissed."

Old man, of course, means pimp.

"Once again, Tanya, how long have you been a working girl?"

"A couple of years."

"You from around here?"

"Yeah. Raised in the Ninth Ward."

"Is the Marriott the only hotel you work?"

"I don't *work* hotels. That's suicide. It's different if my date's staying at one. Tell me, mister, what murder are we talking about?"

"We'll get to that. Let's talk awhile. I want to know about you. You work the streets every night?"

"Not every night. Mostly weekends. Or when there's a special event in town to draw a crowd."

Rice leaned across the desk, resting on his arms and elbows. "Let me tell you something, and listen close. We're homicide detectives. Understand what that means? Homicide. Murder. We don't give a fuck about dope, selling pussy, ripping off tourists, or any of that stuff. Other people handle those problems; we investigate murder. Now, what in hell are you doing with a twelve-inch butcher knife down your boot at three forty-five A.M. in the Marriott Hotel? Are you insane?"

"Protection, man. I've got to have something. I can't walk around like you do, with a gun strapped on."

"Protection from what? Your dates?"

"No, not my dates. Those thieving assholes on the street. Pimps. Other working girls. It's tough out there and, baby, I'm not getting hurt for nobody. Look, mister, I've never cut anyone in my life, but when I first came on the street, I had girls and their old men take my money before I could get in a cab and go home. I ain't layin' on my back servicin' people like a bitch dog so I can get ripped off. Not me."

"Any of your dates ever get rough?"

"Sometimes. But I've been lucky. You ain't lookin' at no fool, baby. I talk to my dates a long time and pretty much know the score before I go anywhere with them. I'm not that strapped for money. My old man takes care of me."

"Have you ever been hurt?"

"Not by a trick."

"What would you do if your date got rough? You just said you wouldn't let anyone hurt you. Maybe you'd use that knife in self-defense."

"I'm not going to get in that position."

"Sometimes we can't control a situation. I've been around a long time. I've seen a lot of you girls hurt by those assholes. I wouldn't blame you a bit if you tried to protect yourself."

"You think I cut somebody, don't you? That's not my style. I just make a little money and go home."

"Tanya, I'm going to tell you what happened. You listen. Keep quiet and listen." *Here it comes,* I thought. I'd seen Rice make it work before. "You pick up an out-of-town trick you thought was solid. You get back to his place, have a few drinks, and take care of business. All of a sudden this dude refuses to pay you. Or maybe you got your money up front and now he wants more time. Either way, this guy turns into a jerk. He starts calling you a whore, a nigger whore, and won't let you leave the room. You don't need this shit, so you push your way toward the door. He—"

"Man, you're crazy."

"I told you, let me finish. Listen. He blocks your exit. Maybe slaps you around a little bit. You pull your knife. You don't want to hurt him. You just want to get out, but this guy's a real asshole. He's drunk. You're scared. All you can think about is getting out of that room. In the same situation, I might do the same thing."

"Do what?"

"Stab him, Tanya, to get out. You had to. Or you didn't have a chance."

"Mister, you're wrong. I didn't stab nobody. When did this stabbing happen? You've got the wrong girl. Let me prove it."

Rice had given her nothing so far, and had no intention of starting. He offered her a scenario, an "out," but she didn't take it. Sooner or later in a drawn-out interrogation, the actual murderer would slip: mention a time, or the Fairmont, or *something* only the killer would know. If Tanya did, we'd pounce.

The goal here was to learn Tanya's whereabouts at 4:49 A.M. yesterday without revealing the time or circumstances of Rodney Robinson's murder.

"Tanya, don't be a damn fool. You have an opportunity a lot of people don't get. Only you can help yourself. I like you, and I don't want to see you spend the rest of your life in the penitentiary just because you had to defend yourself. We know what it's like out there. Help yourself while you can."

"Mister, believe me, if I could help myself, I would. You're talking major jail time. Please believe me, I didn't kill anybody."

"You said you only work weekends?"

"Sometimes I work during the week. But only if there's action. Big things like a convention or a Super Bowl."

"Did you work this last week?"

"I think I worked one day. Monday or Tuesday."

Tuesday: the likely day of the Hines murder. But Mike, rightly, zeroed in on the Robinson killing.

"Did you work the street or hotels?"

"I told you I don't work hotels. Too much heat."

"Did you have a date that night?"

"What night?"

"Monday or Tuesday."

"No. I didn't have my first date until Friday."

When Rodney Robinson died, just thirty-one hours ago.

"What time Friday?"

"A little after midnight."

She meant early Saturday. Today.

"Was that the trick at the Marriott?"

"No. He came later. The first was about one in the morning."

"Tell me something about the first trick."

"Just a guy. He picked me up on Decatur. He has an apartment uptown, somewhere off Carrollton Avenue. A real nice dude. A quickie. The kind I like. Wham. Bam. See you later, Sam."

"And the Marriott trick, he was later, right?"

"Right."

"Well, we know what happened with him."

"Look, mister, I didn't rip him off. He gave me that money. And the knife: it's a bum rap. Those security dudes will do anything to keep us girls away."

"Good luck selling that story, Tanya. But like I said, save it, because we're only interested in one thing. Now let me get this straight. You worked Monday or Tuesday, but didn't get a date. Your first date was Saturday, a little after midnight, with someone who picked you up on Decatur Street. Is that correct?"

"Yeah. Slow week."

"What the hell did you do with yourself the rest of the time?"

"I remember. I worked Tuesday night, and it was dead. Wednesday night I was sick and didn't come out. I worked Thursday night, but it was dragging, so I quit around midnight."

Tuesday night: William Hines could have been murdered Tuesday night. Thursday night: Tanya said she worked until midnight. Rodney Robinson was killed about five hours later.

"What did you do Thursday night? Go home?"

"No. Me and some of the girls went over to Lucky's."

Police have special bars they frequent. So do gay people. And doctors. Lawyers. Downtown office workers. Sailors off ships plying the Mississippi. French Quarter prostitutes also have a favorite watering hole—quite a show goes on there each night—and it's called Lucky's.

"Who were you with?"

"Desirée and Carmen."

"Those their real names or street names?"

"Street names. I don't know their real ones."

"Was Gary tending bar?"

"Yeah," Tanya answered, surprised and impressed. "You know Gary?"

Rice, who seldom drinks, nonetheless knows almost every bartender in the Quarter.

"Sure. Gary's good people. How long did you stay at Lucky's?"

"I don't know. I can tell you the sun hit me in the face when I walked out. It had to be nine or ten in the morning."

So Rice had her alibi for the Rodney Robinson killing. Without divulging pertinent information regarding time and place, we could check out her 4:49 A.M. whereabouts. She couldn't have been murdering Rodney Robinson while drinking at Lucky's. I knew we'd have to go there the next morning, as close to 4:49 as possible, to see if anyone could substantiate her story.

At the property and evidence room—noon, Saturday, November 29—we filled out a form requesting transferral of the butcher knife to the crime lab for testing. The criminalist would locate any traces of blood, however minute, and calibrate the blade, comparing its measurements to the wounds inflicted on the two dead men. He could tell us if the knife's size fit the murder weapon's, and any blood could be analyzed to see if it matched that of the victims. Vital data, but I knew that even with a rush order the lab wouldn't produce its findings until Monday afternoon.

Back at Homicide I found a message to call the brother of a murder victim killed two years earlier. I'd solved the case, winning the brother's gratitude, and he'd phoned me several times since with leads on unsolved cases.

Although we never discussed it, I knew he did drugs. I considered him a valuable informant because of his narcotics connections, but his accuracy wasn't such that I'd drop everything to pursue whatever he said. Four times in the past he called with information; once it led to a killer.

"Pete, John Dillmann."

"Are you handling the murder on Governor Nicholls?"

"Yeah. You hear anything?"

"Maybe. How did the guy get it?"

"Don't you read the papers?"

"Nah."

"Stabbed, Pete. Stabbed a lot of times."

"The talk on the street says a dope deal gone bad. A connection of mine knows the two junkies who ripped him off. It'd be their style, stabbing. I'm supposed to meet my connection tonight. Where can I reach you?"

Hines a pusher? No way. I saw Pete's record falling to one for five.

"Call the desk sergeant. I'll be on the street. I'll get back to you soon as I can."

It's called stroking the informant. Maybe he'd come up with information on another case. Who knew, Pete might have mixed up those drug facts, and still have the right killers. He said stabbing was "their style."

Tyrone Cole loomed largest in my mind, and we couldn't eliminate Tanya Bradford. She fought Susan Graham "like a tiger." But the call from Pete did tilt me in a certain direction, and I knew I'd pursue it shortly.

About this time Homicide commander Steve London, his

young face creased into a frown, waved me and Rice into his office. Heat from higher-ups, I figured.

"John, Mike, fill me in on Robinson and Hines. Are we close yet?"

"Got good leads, Loo," I said.

"That's better than the last time we talked."

I ran down what we knew about Tanya Bradford and Tyrone Cole.

"You still think these cases are connected?"

"Positively," I said.

"I'm not trying to pressure you guys," London said, about to pressure us, "but I have to answer to the Chief; the Chief has to answer to the Superintendent; the Superintendent has to answer to the Mayor; and I'm sure the Mayor answers to the Tourist Commission. Jesus Christ, the Fairmont!"

"There's one consolation," Rice wisecracked. "Robinson could have bled all over the Blue Boom." This was the famous super-exclusive restaurant–supper club where international stars perform in front of elite audiences. The thought made London grimace.

"Naturally," he said, "we're working the weekend. Overtime or manpower, no consideration. Do what needs to be done. Wrap these up."

Our overtime so far had been worked without compensation. That was okay. To think about punching a time clock with a murderer on the streets demanded extreme callousness.

Still, it never ceased to amaze me how politicians, contending the city had run short of money, always insisted that hours needed to be cut back, city workers laid off, municipal services slashed, and so on, because of budget considerations. The police department had labored understaffed ever since I joined it thirteen years before, but let a heater case arise—or something giving tourism a bad image—and money rolled off a handy printing press.

London, a good guy, nonetheless depressed us. We headed to our car and Charity Hospital to interview Alicia Pearson's mother. Alicia was the woman Tyrone Cole lived with.

"Detour through the Quarter, will you, Mike?"

"What's in the Quarter?"

"I want to make a quick stop."

I asked Mike to pull over at the corner of Esplanade and Bourbon, saying I'd be right back. I didn't explain my destination for two reasons. First, no one could know my informant informed—I trusted Mike with my life, but this information he simply couldn't have. Second, I wanted to keep Mike upbeat, to think, as I did, that Tyrone Cole or Tanya Bradford would pan out. I didn't want him believing I was pursuing another suspect without him.

The temperature had dropped steadily in the last three days, and the afternoon was brisk. I walked a block down Esplanade, then turned onto Royal, proceeding to a residence where I met a man I'll call Hollis. Hollis, quite well known, owns a club in the Quarter, and has earned the trust of all kinds of characters.

Hollis owed me, and I doubted a more important case could arise to request repayment. A wealthy and powerful man, he didn't like to be asked, nor did I like asking, but I needed the insider's lowdown on the murders of Hines and Robinson. Was the perpetrator a prostitute? A transient? A strung-out addict trying to make a quick score? Was the motive robbery? Or just a psychopath gone wild?

"I don't know," Hollis said. "But, John, if it's possible to find out, I will."

"I'll see you tomorrow," I said.

Even if Hollis came up with something, it didn't mean we'd solve the case. It did mean we'd have the best information, data that otherwise could take weeks or months to squeeze out.

At Charity Hospital we found Pauline Pearson, Alicia's mother, a nurse's aide, and obtained her daughter's address.

Now for Tyrone Cole. This time we'd find him. We didn't have to put on game faces for Tyrone Cole. He'd shot a man for moving too slowly for his wallet. His own mother lived in fear of him.

⹀7⹀

Gasps of cold, lung-searing November air, punctuated by the organ-jolting force of my feet hitting the ground, gave painful new meaning to "pounding the pavement." I sprinted head-to-head with Rice, five years my junior, sixty feet behind Tyrone Cole, twenty-one to Mike's twenty-nine and running like a rabbit.

No dignity derived from this. As a young patrolman I relished a swift chase, but thirteen years had passed, and so had the enjoyment. I maintained good condition for my age, worked out three or four times a week in the police gym, hitting the big bag, lifting weights, but no exercise makes an individual younger or faster. Pride kept me in pace with Rice, but Cole seemed simply uncatchable.

"Tyrone!" I yelled. My God, that *hurt*. "Police!" Yelling doubled the pain. "We just want to talk to you!" I thought my chest would explode from the effort of those seven words.

I wanted to curse Rice, but knew it would hurt too much. Why didn't he do the yelling?

We'd gone two blocks on Tchoupitoulas Street, bordered by the river on our left and small frame houses on the right, full speed at the start but now at a slow marathon pace, gasping, sweating, faces flushed. I wore leather-soled Flor-sheims. Wearing those shoes, Walter Payton couldn't catch Cole. His sneakers gripped the pavement as he sprinted un-constrained in cut-off jeans and a New Orleans Saints T-shirt, a wide receiver on a fly pattern blowing away cornerbacks.

Rice gained a step on me. I dug in, tried to forget the pain, and pulled even with him. Cole extended his lead to a hun-dred feet, found a break in traffic and cut across Tchoupitou-las, jumped railroad tracks fronting the river, and headed for a row of warehouses jammed up against the wharves.

We ran with guns holstered. All we wanted to do, could do, was talk to him. We knew of no warrants for his arrest, and we didn't possess evidence sufficient to bust him as a suspect in the stabbings. His habit of committing crimes near the Fairmont, his generally fitting the description of the man Nedra Boykin saw charging out of the service elevator, and our own lack of leads led us on this chase.

What if we did catch him? We couldn't book him or force him to talk to us. He spotted Rice and me with Alicia at her front door, knew we were cops, and ran. Maybe he also knew we had two murders to pin on him. Just as likely, he simply didn't want to talk to detectives.

Rice and I puffed across Tchoupitoulas, each holding up a hand to halt honking traffic. Cole had ducked behind a ware-house.

Out of breath, arms more tired than legs, we slowed to a humiliating walk and, finally, to a stop on the ties between the rails. We stood there heaving, feeling foolish. Bent over, hands on knees, I said, "Come on, Mike. Let's get off the tracks."

"Get off? I'm gonna lie down across them. A train right now would feel real good."

Embarrassment increased. We had to walk the gauntlet

past the peering eyes of residents of the salt-and-pepper neighborhood who knew we'd failed: no Tyrone Cole in tow.

Alicia Pearson waited on the steps.

"Tyrone's light," Rice said to her. He's gone. "Your boyfriend thinks we came here to pop him. All we want is to talk. Now listen close, Alicia. Neither of you needs heat from the police. When Tyrone gets back, tell the asshole we want to see him. Here's my card. If I don't hear from him in the next couple of hours, you'll have uniforms camped on these steps day and night."

"What do you think?" Mike said as we headed back to headquarters.

"Cole's dirty. Why else would he take off? If he calls . . ."

"*If* he calls. If my aunt had balls, she'd be my uncle. He's not going to call. You can bet your sweet ass we'll be out here at four A.M. kicking his door down."

"Maybe we should let him cool awhile," I suggested.

"Cool? Shit. You saw him run. What are we waiting for? He's our man."

"If we grab him and don't break him, he'll walk out of our office laughing. I couldn't take that, not after that scene on Governor Nicholls. I think we should let him cool and build a case against him."

Mike wanted to nab Cole and crack him. But what if we failed? We couldn't play him like a hooked fish and keep reeling him in again and again. His lawyer would quickly stop that game with a restraining order. Questioning a suspect is, at best, a one-shot deal; no-shot if he invokes his rights.

Rice feared another murder. However, if Cole was our man, he'd been warned we were on to him. He'd sweat bullets in a personal pressure cooker, not knowing *our* bullets were blanks, which I believed reduced the chances of his committing another homicide soon.

But I was merely guessing. Cole might kill again, that very night.

I weighed the possibilities. If we failed, I kept thinking, we blew everything and increased the likelihood of another murder. By letting Cole cool, I meant taking time to search for a witness who could put him with one or both of the victims. Then we'd break him for sure.

We wrestled with another problem: two separate murders, two cases, two detectives with absolute power over their own investigations. I couldn't prevent Mike from collaring Cole, and he couldn't stop me from what he considered a dangerous waste of time. It behooved us to reach common ground.

"Beans, give it a couple of days. Let's try to link Cole with Hines or Robinson to strengthen our position when we do go into him. It will give us a key, a wedge, to open up everything. We might hit the jackpot with prints when we find Robinson's car. Maybe the partials from the scenes will tie him in."

"Right. Wait. You go back and tell London, 'Our prime suspect broke and ran when we tried to question him on the Fairmont murder and the murder of a *Times-Picayune* employee, but I want to wait.' See what he says. I can tell you. 'Bring this asshole in and get a story out of him. He'll have some half-baked alibi we can destroy.' Dammit, John, we catch a new case every night. How much time do we have?"

"As much as it takes. And what if we do destroy his story? He comes up with another one. *If* he hasn't already gotten a lawyer. Physical evidence, Mike. Let's get some hard physical evidence. Then *we* hold the cards."

Years before, working the murder of a honeymoon bride, I popped off like Mike—full of fire and thirsty for results—and older, more experienced heads counseled patience. Then I couldn't imagine ever sounding like them. I wondered if they'd felt as unsure as I did now.

"Okay, Dillmann, you win. We'll check the prints and run background on the victims. If nothing breaks by then, we bring Cole in for questioning."

Two of the six calls waiting for me at headquarters would significantly alter the case's direction.

Hollis phoned back sooner than I'd expected, leaving no name, only a message: "Phone the club."

I made the call from a pay station downstairs near the snack bar. Hollis insisted. He figured all police phones were monitored. In fact, many are taped as a backup to check notes taken from conversations with a witness. Someone doesn't actually eavesdrop. A very large reel of recording tape located in the radio room stored all calls coming into the department, and many (we assumed) going out.

"Let me speak to Hollis."

"Who's calling?"

"John."

"John who?"

"Just get Hollis. He'll know."

"Yeah," a voice said a minute or so later. "Is that you?"

"It's me. Got anything?"

"Yeah. Let me go to my office. You're at that public number?"

"Right."

"I'll call you back."

Hollis probably headed to a pay phone at the coffee shop a few doors from his club. He didn't trust his own phones.

"Mister H?" I said when the phone rang.

"Yeah. You're after a big lumberjack-lookin' motherfucker. He calls himself Big Frank. Hangs around Camp and Julia."

"Skid row."

"Yeah. The jerk's some kind of drifter. A fruit picker. What you call them guys?"

"Migrant workers."

"Right. Migrant workers. That's what he does. Picks fruit."

"What's the deal with Frank?"

"My people say he's crazy. He juices a lot and only eats lemons and lettuce."

I laughed. Hollis didn't laugh back. "Lemons and lettuce?"

"Yeah."

"All you got is a first name?"

"Yeah."

"What else you know?"

"This broad who works for a friend saw Big Frank a couple of hours after the black dude got carved up in the Fairmont. She . . ."

"What's her name?" I interrupted.

"For this, she ain't got one."

"Go ahead."

"This Big Frank cut a lemon in half with a big knife, and when he stuck the blade in his pants, she saw they were soaked with blood. Stupid broad asked him about the blood and almost got her head pulled off. It scared her shitless."

"Where did this happen?"

"A dive on Julia."

"Anything else?"

"Ain't that enough?"

In a way, yes. Hollis had *never* steered me wrong. He wouldn't put me on to Big Frank for just the lemon-slicing story. I needed more information, but I had to walk a fine line with Hollis, who feared anything he told me could lead back to him.

"How big is this guy?"

"They tell me six and a half feet. Tips the scales at about two fifty."

Not hard to find. But—the old joke came unwanted into my head—what would we do when we found him?

"Tell me more, Hollis."

"You're the cop. I'm not. You want to know who's stabbing those people. I told you. Maybe he jacked them. Maybe
he knew them. Maybe he's just mean. Who knows? This jerk
scares all those wineheads to death. Steady flashin' that blade.
He's bragged about killing before. I think them lemons pick-
led his brain."

A lemon-and-lettuce-eating drunk capable of the violence
attending the murders of Hines and Robinson certainly deserved attention, especially in view of the source. The man
knew.

"Fred," I called over to Dantagnan when I returned to the
homicide room. He banged away at a typewriter, finishing a
report for the D.A. on a major homicide he'd recently solved.
After working the case several months, he'd obtained a true
bill from his presentation to the Orleans Parish Grand Jury.
A moment of pride for Fred, a *detective*, not just solving a
saloon-fight or a domestic-dispute killing. "Come over here,
will you?"

I told him about Big Frank.

"Let's go find the asshole," he said. Many cops, less eager
for action, would have thought twice about Big Frank. Fred
was ready to roll.

"I can't leave right now. I've got other calls to make."

"What can I do?"

I disliked these scenes. Fred had his own case; I wasn't his
boss, and I knew he treasured time at home with Bea and
the kids. No matter that I stood ready to assist when he
needed a hand, I felt badly about continually going to my
closest friend. But I knew he'd say yes—someone else *might*
say no, and always counting on him had spoiled me.

"I'd like you to run Big Frank through the computer alias
file. Then I need you to go to Camp and Julia. Talk to some
bartenders. See what kind of line you can get. But, Jesus,

Fred, be careful. Stay away from this guy. Don't pick him up.
We don't have anything on him, and besides, you'll be
alone."

"I won't be alone."

"How's that?"

"I'll bring some lemons. If he wants to fight, I'll show him
I'm friendly."

"Like sugar for a horse."

"No, peanuts for an elephant. This asshole's an elephant."

"Stay away from him, Fred," I said when my friend headed
out. Then I turned to the telephone. A Gerald Griffin had
left his number.

"Detective Dillmann," he said, after I identified myself,
"what I have to tell you could amount to nothing, but I
thought I should call."

"What's this in regard to?"

"Two murders in the French Quarter. I didn't know about
them until I read this morning's paper."

He had my attention. "What information do you have?"

"I don't know if this will help, but I'm an offshore oil
worker—a roustabout—working seven/seven." Seven days on,
seven off. "I live in the Quarter, and when I'm off, I occasionally go to the Louisiana Purchase bar. Do you know where
that's at?"

"St. Ann and Dauphine."

"Right. Well, three or four times I met this guy at the
Louisiana Purchase and we drank some beers together. He's
crazy, drinks a lot and swallows pills, so we never got real
close. Anyway, early this morning, he asked me to walk him
to the Detox Center at Charity Hospital. He was messed up
bad. I felt sorry for him. While we were walking, he asked if
I'd heard about the two murders in the French Quarter. I
told him no, that I'd just gotten home from offshore. It was

the strangest damn thing. After he asked about the murders, he starts talking about all the times he's been treated at different mental hospitals. He tells me the Detox Center's the best thing to keep from being held accountable for doing something wrong."

"What does that mean?"

"I can only guess. I got the impression he was trying to lay groundwork to alibi some future criminal defense."

"What else did he say?"

"He asked again if I'd heard about the stabbing at the Fairmont. I hadn't, but later, when I read about it in the paper, I figured I should call the police."

"What's this guy's name?"

"Beats me. I didn't want to know. He's a barroom fighter, real nasty, and plain crazy when he's wired. Hair-trigger temper. Drunk and mean."

"Is he white or black?"

"White."

"What's he look like?"

"About thirty. Medium height, maybe five ten, hundred and eighty pounds. Blond hair, mustache."

"Could you identify him if you saw him again?"

"Yes. He lives in the bars. Stays loaded."

"Mr. Griffin, you realize this could be some nut who heard the news or read the paper."

"Could be. But there was something sinister about him. Terrifying. It wasn't that he brought up the murders out of the clear blue, but he seemed almost amused at his own cleverness in beating the system. No doubt he needed detox, I mean he was filled up heavy-duty. But all he talked about was how a person couldn't be held accountable for his actions when he was loaded, if that condition could be documented."

Not true. Drunkenness or being whacked out on pills during the commission of a crime doesn't serve as a defense.
Insanity does. If he checked into Charity Hospital's psychiatric ward, the story might change.

A tricky situation. After drying him out, maybe they gave
him a psychiatric examination. If he were the killer, I
thought, remembering the Hines murder scene, he could indeed be crazy. Interesting that the subject went to the Detox
Center about 5 A.M. *today*, approximately twenty-four hours
after the Rodney Robinson murder.

"Mr. Griffin, how was this man dressed?"

"Jeans, I think. I didn't pay much attention."

"Did he actually tell you he killed someone?"

"No."

"Did you see any blood on his clothing?"

"No."

"Did you notice scratches on his hands, arms, or face?"

"No."

"Did you see any kind of weapon?"

"No."

"Did they treat him at the Detox Center?"

"I don't know. I left him in the emergency room."

"What time did you leave Charity?"

The subject might still be there.

"I stayed an hour or so."

I took down Griffin's address and told him I'd be over to
see him. I needed a written statement. I didn't have high
hopes that what he related would have much significance,
but who could know? Besides, Griffin, a roustabout, might
not be around later if I needed him. He could get transferred
to the North Sea or the Middle East, and then where would
we be if his information proved important?

Also, I wanted to eyeball Griffin—maybe *he* was a nut.

I drove to Charity Hospital, near the Superdome, fifteen blocks from our headquarters on Tulane Avenue. Crime victims are usually brought here, and all homicide cops know the staff well: nurses, doctors (mostly interns), emergency-room personnel, emergency medical technicians, and order-lies. A camaraderie exists between police and ER personnel similar to that between cop and cop. The efficiency and professionalism used in ER always impressed me when an officer was seriously injured, shot perhaps, and brought in on a Code Three. Uniforms blocked off intersections to clear a path for the ambulance, and the medical trauma team waited out on the ramp at the hospital.

Sherri Wilson, the head nurse on duty in ER, walked me to the admitting desk and asked the clerk for records of everyone brought into Detox this November 29.

"We don't have any," the clerk said. "No one to the third floor today."

"Could I look at the records of everyone receiving treatment today?"

Maybe he'd been seen by an intern but not admitted. But of the fifty to sixty people treated, no patient fitted the description Griffin had given.

I drove to 528 North Rampart, on the fringe of the French Quarter near Louis Armstrong Park, to a big, old, two-story frame house chopped up into efficiency apartments.

"Mr. Griffin," I said, "there's no record of Charity admitting any patient to Detox today."

Griffin looked surprised. Forty-seven years old, he was in good shape—roustabouts always are. I felt immediately that he had told the truth. Besides, why would he lie? The important point, did his information mean anything? The man he escorted to Detox might be a drunken lunatic, or wired on pills, shooting his mouth off about a news article he'd read on the murders or gossip—now running rampant in the Quarter—that he'd picked up.

I drove Griffin to headquarters and took a typewritten and signed statement. A uniform delivered him back to his apartment.

I didn't believe obtaining Griffin's statement ranked as super-urgent, but it had to be taken and the time was right. It was a matter of attention to detail, being careful. I knew of cases lost because extra effort hadn't been expended, and the detective in charge always felt sick, often unable to face his peers for months.

Still thinking about what Griffin had said, my mind kicked out the name John Reilly, a uniformed cop, six feet tall, weighing 220 pounds, who walked night patrol in Jackson Square, and who lived and socialized in the French Quarter. Reilly kept abreast of everything that happened in his neck of the woods. A rough customer, like an old-time beat cop, he'd gained the trust of people in his district. And he lived near Griffin.

The French Quarter has two distinct faces: During the day it's brimming with business people and tourists, often Europeans, who come to hear great jazz, browse through quaint shops, and enjoy perhaps the best food in the country. But late at night, especially after midnight, the Quarter has a different atmosphere, one tainted by prostitutes, pimps, jack artists, and hustlers of every stripe. A world of different environments jammed into the tiny one-square-mile area makes the French Quarter—each little section, each block—unique. The block where the Louisiana Purchase bar sits is one of the worst, and the encyclopedia best describing this spot was housed in John Reilly's head.

It was 6 P.M. when I dialed his number, too early for him to be awake.

"Reilly. John Dillmann. Homicide. I need some help."

"Christ, John, you know what time it is?"

At six in the evening Reilly's biological clock read 4 A.M. I'd awakened him from a deep sleep.

"I'm working the Hines case," I said.

"I knew Bill Hines."

Of course he did.

"John," I said, "I'm looking for a pillhead who bums in the Louisiana Purchase."

"Got a name?"

"No. That's the hangup. But I've got a description." I gave it to him.

"I think I've seen him around. He's always fucked up."

"Can you get a name for me?"

"No problem. I'm jam-up with the bartender at the Purchase. I'll talk to him tonight. If I see this asshole, do you want me to put the clamps on him?"

"No. I'm not even sure he's involved. He's running his mouth in the Quarter, but it's probably bullshit. Just see if you can get a name."

"This will cost you a scotch and water."

"Okay." I laughed.

"How can I get hold of you tonight?"

"Call me at home."

Home. I made it to Slidell at 7:30. We lived in a ranch-style, three-bedroom brick house we bought new, a place we were proud of, especially the garden Diane and I had landscaped with azaleas. She worked part-time as a dental lab technician while the kids were in school, and I moonlighted in a security job at the Bourbon Orleans Hotel to make the monthly house payments. Our home was located a block from Amy's Bonne Ecole Elementary School and two blocks from church, a safe, secure place. A school bus picked up Todd right in front of the house for a one-mile ride to Slidell Junior High.

A warm familial scene? Ordinarily, but tonight my Homicide duties upset the domestic applecart for the second time in three days—usually it didn't happen twice in a year.

"Di, I need to get up for work at two thirty in the morning"—the best time Rice and I could meet at Lucky's to check Tanya Bradford's alibi.

"You need some rest."

"Yeah, we're all working extra to catch this killer before he slices somebody else to ribbons. I'll be gone most of tomorrow. Sorry about the picnic." We'd planned an outing at Audubon Zoo with the children on Sunday, my day off.

"Well, we couldn't go any way."

"Why not?"

"Amy's running a fever."

"How high?"

"A hundred and one. Aspirin and rubdowns in the tub help temporarily, but it climbs back up before I can give her more medicine. Bless her heart, she's so cranky and miserable. You know how she loves to cuddle against your chest in the rocker, and I like you here with me when she's sick."

"I'm only a phone call away."

"You're across the lake. An hour away."

"I have things to do."

"Why you? It's bad enough you're at the hotel almost every night during the week. Can't you stay home on Sunday?"

"Sunday is like any other day to murderers, Diane. We have to keep working on this investigation."

"I don't see why someone else can't do it. Amy's sick, and I'd like you to be home."

"How can I control her fever?"

"You don't understand," she said, turning away.

Down deep we both understood: Diane wanted this killer caught; I wanted to stay home. Beneath the surface frustrations and discord our oneness had for a long time been rooted in a much firmer foundation than most cop marriages, and the end wasn't near.

=8=

"**W**hat in hell you doing out this time of morning?" asked a familiar voice outside Pat O'Brien's, home of the famous Hurricane made from 151-proof rum (which can kill you) mixed with several liqueurs and fruit juices.

"Working a case, Jake," I said.

"How about a cup of java?"

I glanced at my watch. I had ten minutes before meeting Rice at Lucky Pierre's in the next block. "Sounds good, Jake. O'Brien's coffee is hard to beat, and I need some bad."

Even Diane, who hates bars, loves Pat O'Brien's live entertainment. This French Quarter landmark pours more booze from its five bars than any other nightclub in the country. Often patrons wait in block-long lines during peak hours.

"Go on inside," Jake said. "I'll fetch you a cup."

"You don't have to do that."

"I want to."

While waiting at a corner table for the coffee I hoped would wake me up, I thought about Jake Miller, a friend and hero to me and many others in and outside the department, one of NOPD's most highly decorated officers, and an admirable, fascinating New Orleanian.

Jake, canine cop, took a German shepherd puppy named Rebel and trained him, with patience and love, into the most honored police dog in the United States.

An avid weightlifter, Jake instructed other cops, myself included, in the police gym. With the looks and build of someone off a Marine recruiting poster—five feet eleven, 220 pounds of solid muscle, big chest veeing into a narrow waist— no one maintained better physical condition than this former defensive back with the NFL's Cincinnati Bengals.

Except perhaps Rebel. Under Jake's strict muscle-toning regimen, Rebel ran, pulled sleds, ate a special diet.

Jake and his partner apprehended felon after felon. Hardly a week went by that they didn't execute some spectacular arrest. Their fame spread from New Orleans to all of Louisiana to the whole nation, to Washington, D.C., itself, where President Richard Nixon feted Rebel—Jake at his side—in a special White House ceremony.

Jake and Rebel shared something close to a father-son relationship, I thought. The unmarried Jake lived with the dog; the two were inseparable.

Every Christmas Day Jake tried to swim the twenty-six miles across Lake Pontchartrain, and once he came within two miles of succeeding. Rebel himself swam the Mississippi River.

Quiet, reserved, likable, Jake always extended a helping hand, especially to the Hospital for Crippled Children. He donated so much money to handicapped kids that he had to work on the docks, unloading ships, to meet his pledges. Jake urged fellow officers to contribute, and we found it impossible to resist.

As for Rebel, off duty the big brown shepherd was a pussycat. I played with Rebel and had no reservations about allow-

ing my son, Todd, to romp with him at a park in games of
fetch and rolling around in the grass. Rebel was a lot of fun,
and you couldn't miss the intelligence in his dark eyes. He
never showed the hostile, snarling, ferocious face felons saw
unless ordered to by Jake.

This revered police dog didn't sniff out drugs or pull crowd-
control duty, "sissy" jobs neither animal nor master wanted.
Instead Jake and Rebel entered dark buildings at night to
flush out armed, dangerous perpetrators. Outside a warehouse
I once saw thirty policemen waiting for Jake and Rebel to
arrive.

The dynamic duo's job ranked among the most perilous
the NOPD offered. Day after day, year after year, Jake and
Rebel apprehended more violent criminals than a whole
squad of police.

But then this most honored police officer, for that's how
we thought of Rebel, was shot and killed in the line of duty
when, as he had done so often, he invaded a darkened building with his master.

Jack simply fell apart after Rebel died. Some of the bounce
went out of his step, and he never got another dog. At his
own request, Jake went back on patrol and continued to in-
struct in the police gym.

When he sat down with me for coffee this early Sunday
morning inside Pat O'Brien's, he was moonlighting working
security, a bouncer in a police uniform. Because his own needs
were minimal, I knew the extra money he worked for would
go to handicapped children.

Lucky Pierre's, on Bourbon Street between St. Ann and
St. Peter, featured back-to-back bars, one serving the dimly
lit club, the other, an open-air courtyard. Across Bourbon
Street from Lucky's stood the elegant Bourbon Orleans Hotel
where I served as director of security, a job difficult to devote

adequate hours to when the murders piled up, which was often. Both the Bourbon Orleans, a former Ursuline convent, and Lucky Pierre's, housed in one of the Quarter's oldest buildings with a wrought-iron balcony overlooking Bourbon Street, qualify as musts for tourists.

Inside, Lucky's featured red satin wallpaper, brick walls, and local celebrity Frankie Ford—the best in the world performing at a piano bar. I stopped for a moment (who wouldn't?) to catch a few bars of his hit song, "Sea Cruise."

At 4 A.M. the front bar, which caters mainly to tourists, had slowed down. A smattering of prostitutes, cops, businessmen—four of them with hookers—and two couples enraptured by Frankie Ford's talent were there. The courtyard bar in back was a current in spot for locals and night people: vice cops, uniforms, off-duty hookers, off-duty bartenders, gamblers, and club owners.

Every city has a place like Lucky's, somewhat seedy, smoke-filled, serving great breakfasts, capturing its essence as Lucky's captures the essence of New Orleans and the French Quarter. The cops keep out misfits and maniacs, employing a strange selection process, and somehow establish a truce. The cops don't bother the hookers, and vice versa.

I found Rice in the courtyard drinking coffee with two First District uniforms. Gary, tending the bar in front, said he'd join us on his break. We didn't want to question him inside with everyone listening.

Gary came back to our table, in about ten minutes, drink in hand. Slender, popular with women, he had a full head of wavy hair, never a strand out of place. Customers said he was a born bartender: efficient, personable, fast. Gary didn't miss a thing, and we felt confident he'd remember if Tanya Bradford had been here, as she said, from midnight on Thursday to 9 A.M. Friday, the time of the Robinson killing.

"Buzzin' in the front, huh, Gary?" Rice said.

"All night, Mike. First time I've sat down in hours."

"Want something to eat?"

"No thanks, got to get back in a few minutes."

"Have you seen Tanya lately? Has she been working?"

"I heard she's in the lockup. Got popped at the Marriott last night. The girls tell me she ripped off a trick. Funny. That's not her style. Goes to show you never know."

"Did she pick that trick up here?"

"No. I haven't seen her since Friday morning. She came in with a bunch of the girls and got all screwed up."

"Working or partying?"

"Strictly play."

"What time did she come in?"

"I came on at midnight, and she hit the front bar about a half hour later. She bounced back and forth to the courtyard bar, still going strong when I left at eight that morning. What's this all about, anyway?"

"Just checking her story, Gary. I'm handling a stabbing at the Fairmont."

"I heard about that."

"Tanya was popped holding a serious knife."

"No way, Mike. She was loaded to the gills Friday morning."

Scratch one suspect. I knew the criminalist's report comparing the wounds on Rodney Robinson to Tanya Bradford's knife would prove negative.

That left three others: Cole, the pillhead in the Quarter, and Big Frank. I told Mike about the latter two after Gary returned to work.

"Who's your choice?" Mike said.

"Big Frank." I couldn't tell Mike who put me on to him, and he had enough smarts not to ask, but to me, Hollis's information was gold.

"How," Mike asked, "does a six-six peach picker stroll

into the Fairmont, butcher a guest, and walk out unnoticed? You weren't on scene, John. Everything was red, like the set of *Friday the 13th*, Jason Voorhees and all. The killer would have been dripping with blood. And what about the security guard? She couldn't have mistaken a small black flash for a white gorilla like Big Frank. I think Cole's our man. Don't forget, he ran from us."

How did *anyone*—black, white, or green—get into the Fairmont? We didn't have the answer. Surely, though, Robinson and the murderer entered the hotel together, went to the room together. Why didn't security spot the would-be killer? Big Frank would stand out in a three-ring circus. The addict Griffin told me about, or Cole, also would draw attention in the sedate Fairmont. I doubted they came decked out in evening clothes.

This Sunday promised much legwork, the tiring nuts-and-bolts grind every detective hates. Adrenaline pumps when you catch a killer or anticipate finding eye-opening evidence, but Mike and I faced nothing this fascinating.

In a way, bureaucracy and the five-day workweek stymied our investigation. We wouldn't have the criminalist's report until Monday, findings for which we held high hopes. But we couldn't take Sunday off to wait on a prayed-for bombshell.

A Wednesday-morning murder compounded by a similar Friday-morning murder. Now, Sunday morning, we sat amid French Quarter characters sipping coffee while, perhaps, a desperate victim screamed in another part of the city.

Mike and I went to the homicide room, its gray color scheme more depressing than usual, and wrote up our dailies on the separate murders we handled. While I tried to figure out if 7:30 A.M. was a good or bad time to give Reilly a call, Fred Dantagnan plowed into the office. Sunday was a day off for him, too, and here he was.

"Morning, Monk. I see you're in one piece."

Fred looked at me, grumbled, then said, "Big Frank's a wuss. We became good friends. He's coming over in an hour to talk with you. I want you to fix Big some lemonade."

"You're kidding."

"Swift, Dillmann." Fred rolled his eyes toward the ceiling. "Think your killer's gonna walk in, put his feet up on the desk, and spill his guts to make your job easier?"

"What about Big Frank?"

"Hold on a minute. My back hurts. Carrying you for thirteen years has caused permanent damage. Wonder if workmen's comp will cover that."

I sat and waited while Fred poured himself a shot of coffee and continued.

"If Big Frank didn't kill Bill Hines and Robinson," he said, taking a seat across from me, "he's definitely an item number waiting to happen." Item number: homicide-case identification tag. Fred guessed that if Big Frank hadn't already killed, the time approached. "The guy's a total fruitcake. A drifter. He picks up odd jobs between binges. Been arrested—his name's Francis Graney—all over the country. Bullshit stuff, mostly fights. He wins them all. Also, disturbing the peace. Drunk in public. Weapons arrests, all involving knives. Popped twice here, both times for fighting."

Fred swallowed some coffee and sighed contentedly. "I hit Camp and Julia yesterday. Everybody on the row knows him. That shit about the lemons is true. This guy's a world-class guzzler. Wine. Beer. Whiskey. Anything. He's a loudmouth who intimidates people. Lives in a flophouse on Magazine Street. Been there about four months. When he's sober, he works for Manpower, the labor pool."

"Did you eyeball him, Fred?"

"No. He was probably sleeping one off."

"Has he been bragging about cutting somebody? Anyone seen blood on his clothes?"

"I didn't dig that deep for fear of spooking the guy. He's still got the knife, though. A bum I talked to in the Hummingbird saw him with it yesterday." Fred took another sip of coffee. "You want to scoop him?"

"Not yet." Fred looked disappointed. "He's one of three. Mike thinks it's Tyrone Cole. I'm leaning toward Big Frank, and then there's a pill-popper Reilly's checking. We're not ready to scoop anybody yet. You got a picture of Graney?"

"Yeah. A mug shot and his arrest register. I put them both in the case file."

"Robinson's or Hines's?"

"Hines. That's yours."

I didn't think it mattered. We had *one* murderer. It *had* to be the same perpetrator. Impossible, I told myself again, for separate killers with the same macabre M.O. to exist in one city.

"What's on the agenda for today?" Fred asked.

"First I'm gonna call Diane. She's pissed. Amy had fever last night, and I met Rice at Lucky's."

"What's the matter with Amy?"

I wanted to bite my tongue. Fred, my daughter's godfather, long ago interpreted his duties toward Amy as going far beyond the ceremonial. Most of the time I appreciated his genuine concern for her welfare, but right now it fueled an already volatile situation.

"Probably just a virus," I said.

"Get your ass home. Mike and I'll cover for you. No problem. Just tell me what you need."

"Let me call first. She's probably out playing in the yard."

"Di," I said into the phone. Mr. All-Ears hovered over me. If I'd had any intention of behaving as less than a proper husband and father, the presence of the powerful, barrel-chested Dantagnan—a family man to the soles of his feet, an adopt-a-family type (he chose mine to adopt)—chased the idea away. "How's Amy?" I wished Fred would move back and give me room.

"Her fever broke for a while early this morning, but now it's back over a hundred. She's real cranky, John. All she wants is for me to hold and rock her. I can't get anything else done. When are you coming home?"

"Have you called the doctor?" I didn't want to answer her question. Fred would hear and order me out. Kids get sick all the time, I told myself.

"Not yet. If it goes higher, I will. When are you coming home?"

"What do you think?"

"Come as soon as you can, John. But it's no emergency. I know how involved you are with this case. You won't be out all night, will you?"

"No."

"Stay if you think you should, John."

"Call me when anything changes with Amy."

I hung up and faced Fred's glare. "Amy okay?" he said, making it sound like an order.

"Still running a fever, but Di's taking her to the doctor in the morning. Everything's under control. *You* go home. I'm ruining your day off, too. Diane's already on my back; God forbid Bea joins forces with her."

Fred interrogated me on his godchild's condition. "Maybe I should call Di myself?" he finally said.

Geesus.

"Go home, mother hen."

When he did, still suspicious, a few minutes later, I called Reilly. "Reilly, John Dillmann, you do any good?"

"Not bad." The street-smart French Quarter beat cop sounded wide awake. "Your guy showed up in the Quarter a few months ago. He's strung out bad, John. Pills. Valium. Quaaludes. PCP. Anything he can get his hands on. What's worse, he juices on top of the pills. The locals call him Crazy Johnny, and the name fits."

"Why's he called Crazy?"

"Several joints have barred him for fighting, which he does often, for no apparent reason. He's a loser, John, just like hundreds of others down here."

"You got a last name?"

"I'm working on it."

"Where's he living?"

"I'm working on it."

"Does he carry a knife?"

"No one I talked to ever saw him with one. He's tough, John. Only real badasses get barred from these places. You won't take him in without a fight."

Wonderful, I thought, *trying to bring in a suspect isn't getting any easier.* Tyrone Cole had run Rice and me into the ground; Fred said Big Frank was a walking time bomb; and now Reilly told me I could expect a no-holds-barred fight with Crazy Johnny.

"Can you get more on him tonight? I really need a last name."

"Listen, do me a favor. I'm working in Jackson Square and doing unpaid overtime looking for your guy. Why not see if you can get me detailed to Homicide for a couple of days?"

"I'll make some calls and give it a try. But we don't have anything concrete yet on Crazy Johnny."

Actually, I liked Reilly's idea and couldn't imagine Steve London turning down the request. No homicides had higher priorities than these, and Steve was getting antsy from placating too many interested parties trying to get a fix on our progress.

It would work out for everybody. Reilly wanted the feel of wearing a suit, rather than a uniform, in what most police officers believe is a prestige job in Homicide. A number of retired officers I know, when they're drinking in bars, perhaps, or chewing the fat and trying to impress someone, will say they worked Homicide. They didn't, but it's not a serious lie, just a harmless fantasy.

Once off the phone with Reilly, I ran the name Crazy Johnny through the alias computer—zip. Years before it would have taken two or three days fighting through thousands of index cards to check on such an alias, but now we got an answer in minutes. NOPD went to computers about the time I joined the force in 1967.

Rice had the name and address of Rodney Robinson's grandmother, who called headquarters shortly after learning of the murder, and we visited her home at 10 A.M. this November 30. Kete Camel was sixty-nine years old and lived on General Pershing, a nice, quiet uptown residential area near Audubon Park. Various friends and relatives had collected at her home.

"Mrs. Camel," Rice said, "I understand Rodney was living in Houston."

"That's right, Mr. Rice. Everybody in this family was proud of him. He was so smart. He just made personnel director with the Houston Hilton. We hated to see Rodney move so far away, but it was such a good opportunity for him. What a waste, Mr. Rice." Grief deepened the lines on this old woman's face. Tears gathered in her eyes. Her grandson, surely fighting long odds, had his brief but bright star extinguished at the Fairmont.

"When did you last talk to your grandson?"

"He was here Thanksgiving. He made a special trip from Houston to have Thanksgiving dinner with me and his uncle. It was so good to see him. He didn't leave until about five thirty that afternoon. Oh, God, I wish he'd stayed."

"Do you know where he went when he left your home?"

"To visit a friend by the name of David, I think. Rodney

said, 'I'll see you tomorrow, Grandma,' when he walked out the door.''

A sob interrupted Kete Camel. Mike and I waited.

She swallowed hard and continued, "It's funny, Mr. Rice, Rodney has his own place in the back of my house. A nice little apartment. I wish he'd stayed here but, you know, the Fairmont—it's real fancy. I guess it's his age. If I was young, I'd rather stay in a plush hotel than with an old lady like me. Who do you think killed my grandson, Mr. Rice?''

"I don't know, Mrs. Camel. But we'll find out.''

"My grandson was a nice, hard-working young man. He didn't deserve to die like that.''

"Do you know where his friend David lives?''

"No. But I might have the telephone number.''

And indeed she did.

"What about Rodney's car, Mrs. Camel? Do you know where it is?''

"At the hotel, I guess. He drove it to David's house.''

But we knew it wasn't at the Fairmont.

Talking with the families of victims ranked as one of the worst parts of our job. Hardly a day went by that Rice and I didn't see a murder victim, often killed in the cruelest way, mutilated perhaps, but we became partly accustomed to the dead. We never became accustomed to the grief of the living.

"Nice old lady, huh?" Rice said when we returned to the car, edging as close to the maudlin as this tough cop ever got.

"Yeah," I said. "I lived quite a while with my grandparents. I know how much they worry. I can imagine how they'd feel if something happened to me.''

I radioed the desk sergeant at headquarters and asked him to look up the telephone number of Rodney Robinson's friend in the Blue Book, a cross-reference of phone numbers and street addresses. Before talking to David, we wanted to cruise his block, looking for Rodney Robinson's red 1976 Chrysler bearing Texas plates. And since David could be our fourth suspect, a surprise visit made more sense than calling for an appointment.

We had found no evidence of forced entry at Hines's apartment or Robinson's hotel room; both men knew their killer. Instead of a weird, lettuce-eating maniac or a strung-out drifter or a black street criminal, we might have an acquaintance with a major beef against the two victims.

David Hennessey lived on Louis XIV Street in the Lakeview section of New Orleans, a comfortable area near Lake Pontchartrain. We didn't spot Robinson's vehicle.

Hennessey, white, twenty-two years old, called himself a close friend of Rodney Robinson, who he said visited him and his family about 6:30 P.M. Thanksgiving evening, talking and reminiscing. They left together at 10:30 P.M. for Pat O'Brien's, where Rodney planned to meet friends.

"What kind of mood was Robinson in?" Rice asked.

"He was on a real up. He liked his new job in Houston."

"Did he seem worried about anything?"

"Just the opposite. We were partying."

"Who was he supposed to meet at Pat O'Brien's?"

"Some friends. They didn't show."

"Did you stay long?"

"About an hour."

"Was Rodney intoxicated?"

"He had a few drinks, but he wasn't loaded. We were having a good time."

"What happened next?"

"We left the Quarter and drove to Andy Capp's Lounge. You know, it's over on Carrollton Avenue."

"How did you get there?"

"In Rodney's car. He loved that Chrysler."

"Did you meet anyone at Andy Capp's?"

"No. We talked, had a few more drinks, and partied. Just a fun evening out. He was in town for the holiday, and we decided to have a good time."

"What time did you leave Capp's?"

"A little before three. We drove to the Porthole, a lounge by the lakefront. They were about to close, and we didn't go in. Rodney was getting tired, so he dropped me off at home."

"What time was this?"

"Three thirty."

Rodney Robinson had an hour and nineteen minutes to live.

"What condition was Rodney in when he left?"

"High. But not drunk."

"Do you think Rodney would have stopped at another bar on his way back to the hotel?"

"I don't think so. I'd wanted to go in the Porthole and have another drink, but Rodney was beat. Said he was going back to the hotel and crash."

"You didn't go back to the Fairmont with Rodney?"

"I told you, he dropped me off here."

"Did you ever visit him in that Fairmont hotel room?"

"No. I've never been there."

Maybe fingerprints taken from the scene would prove otherwise. Again we waited on the criminalist's report, due tomorrow.

"Do you know where Rodney parked his car?"

"I have no idea. Haven't you found it?"

"Your prints should be inside that vehicle, right?"

"I guess. I was in it."

"But you didn't visit his room?"

"Positively not. He brought me home, like I said."

"Robinson leaves you at three thirty in the morning and a little more than an hour later gets stabbed to death in New Orleans's most exclusive hotel. It doesn't take an hour and change to drive from Lakeview to the Fairmont. More like twenty minutes, right? What do *you* think happened? Is it possible Rodney didn't go directly back to the hotel, Mr. Hennessey?"

"Could have been any number of things. Rodney was a great guy. Maybe he picked up a hitchhiker. Maybe he was robbed. Who knows?"

"That's a good question. Somebody knows the answer." Rice hesitated. "Can you tell us anything else that might help? Did Rodney have enemies? Did he owe anybody money? Was he dating somebody else's girl? Anything at all?"

"No. This is just crazy. I go out and have a good time with a friend and wake up to learn he's been murdered. It doesn't make sense."

"Have you heard Rodney," I said, intervening for the first time, "speak of someone named Bill Hines?"

"I don't think so. Who's he?"

"It's not important." But it was.

Driving to headquarters, Rice and I digested Hennessey's story. If it was true—we intended to bring him in for fingerprinting—Rodney had only an hour to live after he got back to the hotel. Returning to the Fairmont ate up the nineteen minutes.

What happened in that hour? Tyrone Cole, maybe. Another thought presented itself. Perhaps Cole had hidden on the Fairmont's tenth floor, waiting for a guest to show up, grabbed Robinson, forced him into his room, killed him, and robbed him. Did he also steal the car?

What about Crazy Johnny and Big Frank? Could Hollis really be so off base?

Signs pointed increasingly to Cole. A black man ran out of the back entrance of the Fairmont shortly after the murder. That's how he got out, I had to believe. We still didn't know how he got in.

I dropped Rice at headquarters and drove across the Causeway, at twenty-six miles the longest twin-span bridge in the world, to get home to Slidell. Everything told me Cole was right, but I didn't believe it.

Amy's fever was up. I called Dr. Sadler. "The smaller the child, the higher the fever," he said. "Watch her closely, give her baby aspirin, and come in first thing in the morning."

Amy slept fitfully. We hovered near her bed most of the night. Before dawn we sat in the bedroom, Diane in a chair rocking Amy, me on the floor telling her about the case.

"Maybe I made a mistake by talking Mike out of picking up Cole."

"You know what you're doing, John. It will be all right." She reached out and put her hand on my shoulder.

≡9≡

"**I** found Robinson's vehicle," said Rice at my desk before I settled into the chair Monday morning. He brandished a dozen sheets of paper—the criminalist's report?—and wore the eager-beaver expression detectives get when a murder seems ready to break.

"When did you find it? Where?"

"This morning about two. The Fairmont vicinity. I saw the vehicle in the nine-hundred block of Common Street, right by Sears, Roebuck. I ran an MVR check, then had it towed to the crime-lab cage. Jim Ducas dusted it inside and out."

It didn't surprise me that it had taken so long to find the car. The Fairmont area is a hub of business and tourism, and the lots and the streets are always packed with cars, which seem to change hourly.

"Any prints on the vehicle?" I asked.

"Three partials and a palm. We're checking them against Cole and Graney. Hennessey's coming in this morning. We'll compare his prints to those in Robinson's room."

"Sounds like you did good, Mike."

"I wonder about the location of Robinson's vehicle: a

block and a half from the Fairmont. Why didn't he pull into the hotel parking lot? That's a business district. He wasn't stopping somewhere for a nightcap. No bars."

Maybe, I thought, he didn't want to pay the $6 parking charge, decided to leave the car legally on the street, and walked the block and a half. Maybe he got jacked by Cole during that short walk. Still, how did they *get in* without being seen?

I looked at Mike, a smile still on his face. "What else you got?" I asked.

"Bigger news than the car, probably. Remember that blue skullcap in the hallway of the Fairmont? Alan Sison in the crime lab found head hairs from a negro male inside the cap."

I let this register. Cole again. I hadn't thought beyond Cole when Steve London came bouncing out of his office.

"How's your daughter? Nothing serious, I hope."

He knew about Amy because I had called to say I'd be late. "Diane can't break the fever. We drove her to the pediatrician this morning. He put her on antibiotics and took a blood sample. The baby's burning up."

"Go back home. I'll put Fred on the case with Mike."

"Let me wait for the results of Amy's blood work this afternoon. I'll talk to you then." Amy and the double murder had put me on such an edge that even the doctor and Diane advised I should attend to the one on which I might contribute something positive.

"I trust you know best," London said, looking skeptical. "But talk to me *now* about these cases." He motioned to Mike and me and headed for his office.

Rice and I sat side by side across the desk from London. "Are we still looking for the same perpetrator in both cases?" he asked.

"Positively," I said. I'd said this before. "There can't possibly be two animals out there using the same M.O."

"Where do we stand?"

"Our prime suspect is Tyrone Cole. A black jack artist. Lengthy record. Always around the Fairmont. We have a security guard who saw a male fitting Cole's description fleeing the hotel about the time of the murder. She can't make an identification, but the description fits."

"You held a lineup?"

"Yeah. I showed pictures. No good."

"What else?"

"Mike just told me Alan Sison found head hairs from a black male in a skullcap outside the victim's room."

"Think we can match those hairs to Cole?"

"We'll try. But last time we attempted to question him, he split and ran."

"You put out a Wanted?"

"Not yet. We have some other suspects."

"Who?"

"A drifter named Big Frank and a junkie called Crazy Johnny."

"Big Frank? Crazy Johnny? Sounds like my old platoon in the Second District." We waited for London to finish laughing at his own joke. "Seriously, how does that pair fit in?"

"Big Frank's name came from an informant. A solid informant, Steve. Frank was seen with a large knife and blood on his pants after the Robinson homicide. The other guy, Johnny, tried to check himself into Charity Hospital Detox Center early the morning after Robinson's murder. We have a witness who says he tried to check in strictly to establish his insanity."

"Detox? Insanity?"

"What's new? Johnny doesn't understand the law."

"Do you have anything else?"

"We did background on Robinson. He visited his grandmother Thanksgiving Day, and partied with a friend that night. They allegedly barhopped until three thirty in the morning before Robinson went back to the hotel."

"Wasn't he killed about four thirty? Maybe his friend went back to the hotel room."

"I don't think so. The kid seems straight."

"You get prints from the room?"

"Some partials. He's coming up this morning to be printed."

"And you're sure we have just one perpetrator?"

"Yes."

"With those hairs found in the skullcap, Cole's probably your man. Why haven't you picked him up?"

"We just learned about the hair."

"Why didn't you put a Wanted out on him when he ran?"

It looked like we should have, and that I had made a major error. London's question reverberated in the room's deafening silence. Rice could have made himself look good by saying, "I wanted to, but I went along with the more experienced Dillmann."

But Mike didn't say a word.

"Well," London finally said, "let's pick up Cole. Try to wrap this mess up. Fairmont corporate headquarters called, and the honchos at the *Times-Picayune* want to know how we're doing."

"Right," I said.

"We're averaging a murder every thirty-six hours. How many active cases you working, John?"

"Five." He'd asked me this question before. But I'd devoted all of the last several days to the Hines/Robinson double whammy.

"And you, Mike?"

"About the same."

"It won't lighten up." London looked at the ceiling. "Go pick up Cole."

* * *

Beans and I sat in the unmarked 1978 Ford LTD on a
deadly dull surveillance routine. Earlier, I'd returned home
to find Amy still feverish and with a rash. Diane, increasingly
concerned, awaited another doctor's appointment in the
morning. Mike, in the meantime, had caught some badly
needed sleep. Now we were parked high on a Mississippi
River wharf, peering across the railroad tracks through
binoculars at the front entrance of Alicia Pearson's house,
some two hundred yards away. Night had fallen on New
Orleans; moonlight sparkled on the water, ships blew their
horns in the silent darkness, navigating downriver to the
Gulf of Mexico or upriver to St. Louis and beyond. We
smelled fish and acrid diesel fuel, sharp scents helping us
stay awake.

Although we figured Cole was still staying with Alicia, we
nonetheless notified the Fifth District watch commander to
have his patrolmen keep eyes peeled for him at his mother's
place in the project. I doubted if he'd go there. He shouldn't
come to Alicia's, either.

Detective fiction often portrays very clever killers, but real-
life criminals are rarely shrewd Professor Moriarty types who
plan for months, think out every move, and befuddle the
police with ingenious schemes. The simple truth is, many of
them are pathetic, albeit dangerous, nitwits acting on impulse, spurred by an immediate need for money, drugs, sex,
whatever.

Nevertheless, opposed by a hopelessly overworked police
force, killers would enjoy a skyrocketing success rate if they
kept quiet. But they don't. The vast majority of them talk,
run their mouths to someone, most of the time bragging about
what they did. Why they think a murder calls for boasting is
beyond me.

What Cole *should* do, if he killed William Hines and Rodney Robinson, was follow the advice of a good lawyer. It was likely that we would never convict him.

What he'd *probably* do, if guilty, was continue life as usual. Of course, he knew we looked for him, but he hoped we wouldn't come back. The police always come back, but hope in the suspect's mind becomes belief as a rationalization process kicks in, and the perpetrator soon gets picked up.

A lawyer would tell the suspect, "Here's my card. If you're stopped by the police, say only that you want your attorney present. Say nothing else. Then call me."

Instead, the perpetrator brags to his cohorts, characters like himself, who in a heartbeat will sell him to the police for expected leniency in a case of their own, cash rewards (I've seen murders over half a bottle of wine—imagine what they'll do for $500), or personal retribution for some real or imagined offense.

The people talked to talk. If the killer tells four people, they tell four—sixteen, and each of these blab to four—sixty-four. The first boast is a pebble tossed into water that ripples, spreads, until it inevitably hits shore: the investigating detective.

"Seen anything at all?" Rice asked. We'd passed the binoculars back and forth for two hours.

"No movement. Nothing."

"Think he's there?"

"Yeah. Probably curled up in bed watching the late show while we sit out here freezing."

"Any lights on inside?"

"In the back."

"Let's hit the house. My ass is numb from sitting."

I went to the front, Mike to the rear. Likely he'd get the action when I knocked.

I gave Rice time to position himself, then banged hard on

the door so anyone inside would know who knocked—the police, not a visitor, a burglar, or a drug dealer. The pounding, authoritative sound helps establish control right away. Besides, if Cole chose to rabbit again, he'd run right into Mike's arms.

Alicia Pearson, dressed in housecoat and slippers, opened the door.

"Alicia," I said, "tell Tyrone to come out. I want to talk to him."

"He's not home, mister."

"Where is he?"

"I don't know. In the street, I guess."

"Mind if I take a look?"

"No. Look all you want. He's not here."

I walked into the living room of the house, holding my service revolver at my side, and went front to back, flipping on lights. When I reached the rear I yelled to Mike, "It's me," and let him in.

"Nothing, huh?"

"Doesn't look like it. Let's check again."

Together, peering under beds and into closets, we retraced my steps.

"I told you he wasn't here," Alicia said.

"Did you give Tyrone my card?" Rice said. "Did you tell him to call?"

"I gave it to him. But he won't call, Officer. He's afraid."

"Afraid of what?"

"Afraid of the police. You know how many times he's gone to jail."

He sure hadn't stayed in very long. No time at all for shooting that tourist in the stomach.

"Listen," Rice said, "if he's not going to call, you better. Next time he comes home, go to the phone and call me. If you don't, we'll be walking through your house a hundred more times. You don't need this shit, Alicia, and sooner or later we'll find him. You understand?"

"Yes, sir. But I'll have to go down by the grocery to call."

"He won't know it was you."

Talking Mike out of going after Cole had weighed on my mind. A bad move on my part. I wanted to make a comeback.

"Let's swing by the Fairmont," I said, when we got back to the car.

"Why? Think he's sitting in the lobby waiting for us?"

"You never know. Every one of his arrests has been near the Fairmont."

Good sense dictated he stay away, but, as I said, we weren't matching wits with a master criminal. Neither murder, with the excellent chance of close neighbors hearing the victim scream his lungs out, had been planned for maximum privacy.

Cole wasn't lounging in the lobby; he was a block away, on the corner of Canal Street, talking animatedly, jiving with three males who looked like hustlers.

The four spotted us before we saw them. Maybe they knew we were coming. Impossible, of course, but those who spend years on French Quarter streets develop a fine sensitivity to the presence of police. And they can certainly recognize a police vehicle—marked or not. The four men, maintaining a leisurely pace, began splitting in separate directions when they caught sight of us.

Cole headed toward the river on Canal, figuring his best chance lay in not bolting but walking with an easy, natural gait, purposeful enough to indicate a destination, slow enough not to depict flight.

Mike turned left, then made two quick rights so we could catch Cole head-on coming down deserted Canal, in daylight one of the busiest streets in town.

He saw us coming but didn't know why, nor that we were the same pair he outran two days ago. Cole turned casually, averting his face from us in a window-shopping pretense, and what little hope he previously possessed—like a dash across Canal—disappeared. Before the car fully stopped, I came out of the passenger side. Rice slammed it into park and grabbed Cole almost as quickly as I did, the vehicle still rocking behind us.

As we collared him, I yelled, "Don't run, fuckhead. I don't feel like chasing you." The actual words, used to startle and paralyze, were unnecessary, because he had no place to travel except through us. Before he could turn, Mike had one arm, I the other, and we twisted him spread-eagle against the display window. Mike frisked him. No weapon.

We'd come on rough, out of necessity—our own safety—but now we had to back off. Cole was a suspect. *Only* a suspect. We had probable cause to pick him up, but not to arrest him. We carried no warrant.

"Why the hassle, Sarge?" Cole said, his eyes darting from Mike to me. "I ain't done anything."

"You're Tyrone Cole, aren't you?" Rice said.

"That's me."

"Alicia Pearson's your old lady?"

"Yeah. What'd she do?"

"Nothing, asshole. We want to talk to *you.*"

"About what?"

"Later. Right now we want you to take a ride to our office. Any objections?"

"Am I under arrest?"

"No. We just want to talk."

"Do I have to go?"

"You figure it out."

And Cole did. I could almost hear the wheels clicking in his head. We had probable cause to pick him up, bring him

— 135 —

in for questioning, and, of course, he had to come. He *didn't* have to talk to us, and before we advised him of his rights, anything he told us couldn't be used against him.

We didn't clamp on handcuffs for the ride to headquarters. Why alienate him? We wanted to start him talking, he volunteered to come with us, and we needed to keep in mind his suspect status.

For reasons of privacy—the homicide room buzzed with activity—we questioned Cole in Steve London's office. The room featured a desk, several chairs, walls adorned with London's awards, and windows that don't open. I doubt if the windows could be broken with a fist, certainly not by a body trying to plunge through to almost-certain death three stories below.

Many murderers had sat in this room. Numerous dedicated detectives had pulled countless confessions out of killers here.

I was part of the history of this room. Here a son told me how he had contracted his mother's death. Two sixteen-year-olds confessed to me that they had bludgeoned an eighty-year-old widow to death and raped the corpse. And it was here that I listened to the homicide that appalls even Homicide: a kidnapped, battered, murdered seven-year-old abducted by a neighbor recently released from a mental institution as "cured."

I sat behind London's desk facing Rice and Cole, Mike seated between our suspect and the door. We had our feet up on the desk, a gesture informing Cole he now breathed in *our* environment. *We* can do this, *you* can't. *We* can smoke, *you* can't unless we say so. In short, silent intimidation.

Mike offered Cole a choice of coffee or a soft drink before we began. He took the soft drink. We wanted to lower his guard a little bit, knowing that previous arresting officers surely hadn't treated him this way.

Both Mike and I rode an anticipatory high, one an athlete must feel before a big game, and no matter how Cole interpreted our actions, we were out to win. If we didn't break him, he walked out of the office free. That wouldn't make London happy, nor many others in the city. Uppermost and never to be forgotten, the person who slaughtered Hines and Robinson could strike again.

The confession was critical. We had no physical evidence and weren't sure of getting any. There were those hairs in the skullcap, but if he didn't give us samples voluntarily (and why would he?), how could we obtain anything for matching?

Cole sat hunched over, frightened. None of his experiences with police had been pleasant, and he didn't expect a change here. Besides, he'd made his way up to the big time, the homicide room, and he knew it.

"Tyrone," I said, "I'm going to read you your rights, and I want to be sure you understand them. You're a suspect. Do you know what that means, Tyrone?"

"No. Not exactly. I'm not under arrest?"

"A suspect," Mike said, as if perturbed. "You're *not* under arrest. You don't see any handcuffs on your wrists, do you?"

"A suspect," I said, "means we think you might be involved in a crime. It doesn't mean you won't be arrested later."

"Then you think I did something?"

"Exactly."

"What did I do?"

"Listen to your rights: You're a suspect in the murders—"

"Murders!"

"Shut up and listen. In the murders of William Hines and Rodney Robinson. You have the right to . . ." I continued, proceeding to the conclusion of the important *Miranda* warnings. Detectives read them so often—and people like Cole hear them so often—the urge to ignore the ritual intrudes. I've seen criminals go free when that urge is indulged.

Finished, I looked at Cole. "Do you understand these rights?"

"Man, you had me worried. I didn't kill anybody. I didn't even know those two dudes." A smile crossed his face, and his entire hunched-over frame visibly relaxed, the first sign we were in trouble. Cole had big worries about doing *something* wrong, that's why he ran, but whatever that was, he didn't fear murder charges.

I needed to go on. Possibly I misread this first impression— after hundreds of homicides, I doubted it—and of course Cole could be a great actor, or just cocky, assuming no evidence pointed to him.

"Do you understand your rights?" I repeated.

"Yes."

"Are you willing to answer our questions?"

"If they're about those murders, I'll tell you anything you want to know."

"Tyrone, I've reviewed your record. Pretty extensive for a kid your age."

"Chump charges. Mostly bullshit."

"Do you have a trial date?"

"Trial date?"

"Yeah, trial date. Aren't you out on bail? Purse snatching by the Fairmont."

"Oh, yeah. My attorney tells me they're gonna drop those charges."

"What about the shooting in May?"

"All a mistake. This dude got robbed and shot, and they said it was me."

"Mistaken identity, right?"

He smiled. "Right."

Rice fidgeted in his chair.

"And where did the shooting take place, Tyrone?"

"Around Canal Street, I think. That's what they told me."

"Think about it, Tyrone. Wasn't it around the Fairmont?"

"I guess so."

"The obscenity charge. In front of the Fairmont, too, right?"

He didn't answer.

"You work the Fairmont?"

"I don't work at the Fairmont."

I took my feet off the desk and leaned across, looking right at him. My voice rose, "Cut the bullshit, Tyrone! You think I pulled your name out of a hat? You think Detective Rice and I sat around having coffee and out of nowhere decided, 'Let's fuck with Tyrone Cole today'? We've put a lot of assholes like you behind bars. You work the Fairmont. Your mother lives in the project and you and your old lady live uptown. You make your hustles, and the Fairmont is your fishing ground. We're cops and you're a seven-cent thief, so let's cut the crap. Now, I'm going to ask you again, you work the Fairmont, don't you?"

"Yeah." He mumbled. "But I never go inside. Security's too tight. Look, maybe you're right, I work the street. But I didn't kill anybody. Just tell me when these murders happened, so I can get the hell out of here."

He wanted to make an alibi and leave. This interrogation was going less than well, it was falling apart. Mike and I had exchanged several communicative glances, and I knew he'd plummeted as far as I had since the high of grabbing Cole.

"Where were you Thanksgiving?"

"At home. With my old lady."

"Didn't go out at all?"

"For a little while. Shot some pool and drank a few beers. That's all. No hustles."

"What time did you get home?"

"A little after midnight."

"How do you know? Did you look at a clock?"

"Hey, man, let me explain something. My old lady's a square chick who don't understand when I'm out on the street. I come home every night around midnight. If I stay out all night, I listen to too much shit. This woman's the best thing that ever happened to me."

Probably true, but I doubted if Cole appreciated the fact.

"You want us to believe you're tucked away every night in your warm little bed with Alicia, right?"

"Man, you can ask her. Call her right now. She'll tell you. I make my hustles early, then, bomp, I go on home."

"Maybe we should go talk to Alicia."

"Do you have to? She's on my case now. Can't you just call her?"

"Come outside with me a minute, Mike," I said.

"What do you think, Beans?" I asked, once we were out of the room.

"What do I think? I think we're pissing in the wind."

An experienced detective knows when he's on the wrong track, and has the good judgment to switch directions. Pounding forward leads to dangerous collisions down the line. But we'd invested a lot of hope in Tyrone Cole, and cutting him loose meant practically starting over.

"Let me try him," Mike said.

He went in alone to give it everything he had. But we'd *known* when we mentioned murder and Cole smiled.

I went to my desk and called Diane. One-thirty A.M. seems an outrageous time to call your wife, but we'd worked it out years before. She'd rather hear from me and know what I was doing than wake up at four, wonder and worry, and not be able to fall back asleep.

When she told me Amy's fever was up, I said I'd be right

home. Thoughts of my daughter were jumbled with flashes of the case while I waited the few minutes Rice needed to finish with Tyrone.

Big Frank. Crazy Johnny. Amy. My little girl and Crazy Johnny, tangled in the same thought, tangled in a nightmare. Maybe *I* was going crazy.

☰ 10 ☰

I picked up another homicide the next week. John Reilly checked in with startling information about Crazy Johnny. London increased the pressure. Fred and I met Big Frank. And Amy's fever lessened.

The new murder was an unidentified derelict found bludgeoned to death inside the shell of an abandoned slum house. Usually such a victim bummed a bottle of wine, huddled in a building with friends seeking warmth, and got in a fight over the booze. I had to obtain the dead man's name, pinpoint his hangouts, talk with other homeless people, and then, I suspected, visit railroad yards, rousting hobos out of boxcars in search of a suspect who intended to leave town in a hurry.

Reilly, whom London readily detailed to Homicide, met me Wednesday, December 3, at the Bourbon Orleans Hotel, where I directed security. We sat alone in the small, dimly lit lounge—candles on the six tables, ten barstools, a piano— at 11:30 A.M., just before the place opened for business. Reilly sipped a Bloody Mary. He'd been up all night.

The big, broad, husky beat cop, definitely not someone to

mess with, liked to say, "Thirteen years on the force, and I haven't gotten my ass kicked once."

Quite an accomplishment, actually. Many of those years on his rough French Quarter patrol he worked without a radio, having to take care of business himself. Instructors at the Police Academy regaled recruits with stories about Reilly's nightstick expertise—a skill, oddly enough, that probably saved several lives. Ugly scenes develop for a patrolman unable to radio for backup. If he doesn't use the nightstick, he must resort to the gun.

Today Reilly's usual flippant attitude about a terrifying street person ("Ahhh, he ain't nothing") was absent as he told me about Johnny.

"What's the problem?" I asked. "Doesn't anybody in the Quarter know his real name?"

"It's a different world down here. You know that, John. Everybody uses street names. But I'm making headway. Johnny's been popped several times in the Quarter, nothing serious yet. Believe me, it's only a matter of time."

"Is this guy really bad or does he just enjoy intimidating people?"

"He's stone nuts. He picks fights for no reason. He'll jab his finger hard into your chest and say, 'I hate gray shirts; you're an asshole for wearing one.' He'll swing at you at the drop of a hat, and lately he's gotten worse. Now he's using booze, a lot of it, to wash down the dope. From what I understand, nobody can control him. He went walleyed wild at the Mississippi River Landing bar and tore up the place. Six guys tried to hold him until a unit arrived. No way, he broke loose and scrammed. Six guys. Does that tell you anything?"

"Yeah. Tells me he's on some serious dope."

"PCP."

PCP: Angel dust, rocket fuel, elephant tranquilizer, killer weed, cyclones, DOA. PCP has dozens of names, all adding up to the same thing: one of the world's most dangerous drugs, both to the user and to anyone around him.

Horror stories abound about PCP (phencyclidine, originally developed as a veterinary tranquilizer and super general surgical anesthetic). In the early days of its use, surgery patients anesthetized by PCP painlessly watched doctors cut open their chests. Today the drug is cheap to manufacture (dangerous, though: people frequently get blown up making it) and relatively inexpensive to buy.

If Crazy Johnny indeed used this drug, I understood why six men couldn't subdue him: Johnny literally felt no pain and, short of death, couldn't be hurt.

The PCP user may think he's a bird and leap off a skyscraper expecting to fly, or visualize himself as an invincible Superman. In a way he is, because he'll keep attacking through punishment that would slow down a charging rhino. A Washington, D.C., police official, Gary Hankins, pointed out that "A lot of the self-defense techniques our officers use rely on pain. You hit someone in the shin with a nightstick, you hit them on the elbow or forearm, that pain will subdue them. People on PCP are often impervious to the pain. Sometimes an officer will have to beat away on someone like that because he jeopardizes his own life by trying to control the person."

Two stories, culled from a long, horrifying list, suffice to show this drug's monstrous effects. On Christmas night—of all times—a Maryland businessman on PCP decapitated his fourteen-month-old son, proclaiming his child the reborn Jesus who "had to die for everyone's sins."

And then there was Sharon Araoye, twenty-six, in Prince George's County, Maryland, who under the influence of PCP advanced nude toward a police officer. She plunged a butcher knife into her abdomen, took another step, and thrust it into her groin. The cop stood amazed. Araoye stabbed herself in the chest, and still she continued toward the officer. She drove the blade into her eye. Finally, mercifully, as she lurched for the cop, her intended target, he shot her three times. Araoye died five hours later.

I've heard several NOPD officers tell how much they dread confronting someone strung out on PCP. Taught to use only the force needed to counter resistance, they almost have to kill the individual using the drug.

"Reilly," I said. "Does Johnny have any other reported instances of violence besides the Landing?"

"Ten or twelve, and I've just begun. I'm talking serious fights."

"Sounds like he's capable of the bloodbath I saw at Hines's apartment."

"Take it to the bank."

"What do we need, Reilly? This is your turf. You can't tell me Crazy Johnny's terrorizing the Quarter, been barred from a bunch of dives, and no one knows his name."

"I've got several things cooking. For one, I'm meeting a guy at five—name's Craig Masters—who Johnny smashed a couple of months back. One of the few times our boy got popped. Surely Masters will know the date and location of the fight. With that I can check the trip sheets at First District station and find the arrest number and ID. And second, I'm trying to set up a meeting with a French Quarter joint owner I've known for years. He barred Johnny and gave his bartenders orders to call the police immediately if Johnny set foot inside the bar. I've tried to talk to him, but he's avoiding me. He knows about something a lot more serious than any bar fight."

"Let's get together later today," I said. "The interviews sound promising."

I wanted that name badly, to get an arrest record and photograph. If right now I saw Crazy Johnny walking down the street, I wouldn't recognize him. With a picture, Griffin could ID him, and we'd have probable cause to pick him up. All I had now was a PCP freak fighting a lot in the Quarter.

"Bad idea," Reilly said. "Everybody here knows me. They'll talk to *me*, but a new face will spook them. Let me set it up. I'll call you."

Steve London wanted to see me. I sat down in the "hot seat" where Tyrone Cole had cleared himself, curious about what London had to say. Unlike some police commanders, who handed a detective a case and said, "Let me know when it's solved," Steve had a hands-on policy, offering a good ear and, often, helpful advice and suggestions—tools I certainly could use now.

"John," London said. "you and I go back years. We've worked cases together, and I don't have to tell you how much I respect your abilities. But I have to be honest. I'm concerned about you. You don't look good."

"I'm all right."

"You still working your detail?" The security job at the Bourbon Orleans.

"Hell, yes. I have to."

"How about your daughter? Is she any better?"

"The doctor put her on a new antibiotic. The fever's down but still lingering." I hesitated, wondering about this unusual dialogue. "What's going on, Steve? Did I do something wrong?"

"On the contrary. I'm just worried about you burning out."

"I'll be happy to take a month's vacation." I laughed, but in a sense I didn't really want the time off. My worry about the case would only increase with the investigation out of my hands.

I knew what London meant by "burning out." The average career of a homicide detective is three years, at which point he often becomes hopelessly irritable, cynical, and dis-illusioned. He's hardened. He loses his investigatory fire, does minimal work to draw his paycheck, and hopes fervently that murders will simply stop and he'll never be assigned another.

The best homicide detectives are not only thoroughly pro-fessional but also fresh, eager, and intense, filled with the feeling they can make a difference. Experience counts strongly, but a Catch-22 often intrudes: by the time a detec-tive acquires experience, he's burned out.

I'd put in nine years as a homicide detective. London held the job for three before acing all those tests that got him to his present high position of commander—probably just an-other way station in the hierarchy for him.

But I suspected that three years of street level, down and dirty homicide investigation was about all Steve would have, or perhaps could have, endured. So many dead bodies viewed—almost obscenely—up close and personal can easily become a continual nightmare of gore and depravity that few people can cope with very long.

I didn't think I'd burnt out. *Intensity*, the key to it all, I still possessed. And experience. Most important, I didn't dread going to work. I looked forward to new challenges, hoped I'd draw the toughest cases, and believed my job did make a difference. Like the current investigation: I had no doubt that someone's life, maybe several lives, depended on our collaring this maniac.

But I had to admit *I* might not sit as the best judge of what I did or didn't suffer. I'd seen other homicide detectives, con-fident they could go on forever, transferred to desk jobs in Auto Theft or the day shift in Burglary.

"If we could afford a month off," London said, "I'd gladly give it to you. But you know the department's snowed un-der."

"I know we're busy. Now tell me, what's the problem?"

"It's not a problem, but you have a full caseload, a regular detail, your daughter's sick, and it looks like the Hines case is falling apart."

"What makes you think it's falling apart?"

"You struck out with Tyrone Cole, didn't you?"

"Sure we did. But that's not the end of the investigation. We still have a psycho out there who killed two people."

"And you're sticking with the one-killer theory?"

"How many times do I have to say it, Steve? One guy. Cole doesn't change a thing."

"You're standing in a minority." He let that sink in. The consensus in Homicide—all but me, Rice, and Fred—judged that we dealt with separate killers. "I understand your two chief suspects are white."

"Listen, Steve, we have a security guard at the Fairmont who says she saw a black male run from the building about the time of the murder, and maybe she did. But maybe the commotion from Robinson spoiled this guy's plan to commit a crime in another part of the building. Sure, it's a farfetched coincidence, but we've seen stranger. The bottom line is that she can't make an identification and her description is vague."

"What about the skullcap? The negroid hairs in it?"

"Could be anyone's. Our men found that cap in the hall fifty feet from the murder room."

"Which one of the remaining suspects are you targeting?"

"Francis Graney."

"What about this Crazy Johnny?"

"He's not out of the picture. The guy's a PCP freak, certainly capable of these killings."

"Why Graney?"

"My informant, Steve. He hasn't been wrong."

We'd been through this before. Although some courts had disagreed and jailed policemen who refused to reveal a source, the widespread feeling in law enforcement holds that a cop and certain of his sources possess the same confidentiality accorded a lawyer and client. Prohibiting the police from assuring anonymity to some top informers would make our job inestimably more difficult, and the crime rate much higher.

"Do you have enough to pick Graney up?"

"Nowhere near enough. But, now with Cole eliminated, we can concentrate our efforts more on Big Frank."

"What's your plan?"

"A lot of background. If it confirms my suspicions, we'll have to go get him. Hell, Steve, this case is a bitch. No eyewitnesses and, as of yet, no physical evidence. Without a confession, we're looking at the bottom drawer."

"What about Reilly? Any help, or should we send him back to the District?"

"Leave him detailed for a while. He should have a name on Crazy Johnny soon, then I can decide on his eligibility as a suspect. Look, Steve, I'm okay. I'm just tired."

"Do you need more men?"

"No. Rice is on it full-time, and Dantagnan's my right arm."

With Crazy Johnny on hold because Reilly hadn't yet set up a meet with either the frightened club owner or the man who duked it out with Johnny, at 3 P.M. Monday, December 8, Fred and I found our way to Camp and Julia in search of Big Frank. Skid row—about ten blocks from the French Quarter in the Warehouse District near the Greater New Orleans Bridge that connects New Orleans to Algiers on the east bank.

Later all these warehouses and dilapidated buildings were bulldozed for the 1984 World's Fair. In 1980, however, the truly destitute and lost of New Orleans made the streets and empty buildings around Camp and Julia their home. The Bowery in New York and parts of State Street in Chicago are the counterparts of the Crescent City's Camp and Julia area. It's the end of the line; a sad, depressing place where no one lingers, except an occasional cop investigating a crime, and the homeless.

On some of the corners stood bars catering to people who beg money for a drink and an occasional longshoreman or two. Cheap flophouses abound (often not cheap enough), and a few soup kitchens, too.

Why had it taken until December 8 to get here? Well, the investigation of the bludgeon murder in the abandoned slum house—conducted hurriedly because the killer was likely to skip town—had led to an arrest. But it took time, time taken (necessarily, because it was the more recent of the murders) from Camp and Julia and learning what we could about Big Frank. But eventually, this day of the celebration of the Immaculate Conception, we found time to do background on Big Frank.

Fred and I wore jackets and ties under overcoats needed against a wet, cold winter wind blowing off the Mississippi. People almost oblivious to our presence and their own sat on curbs and doorsteps, gazing at us with unregistering eyes. We parked our unmarked unit on Camp; no need to play cat and mouse here; we had no chance of coming across as anything other than cops.

In the first dive we entered, the grimy, unshaven bartender would have appeared equally at home on the other side of the bar or loitering in the street, except that a spark of life flickered in his eyes when he saw us. His four or five customers, hunched over glasses of warm, flat beer, didn't stir.

"Know this guy?" I said, flipping a B of I photo onto the bar in front of him.

"Yeah," he said, not removing the unlit cigar butt from the corner of his mouth. "Big Frank, a regular lately."

"Come on down to the end of the bar. I want to talk to you."

He lumbered slowly, unnoticed, away from his patrons.

"What can you tell me about Big Frank?" I asked, once Fred and I had him alone, so to speak.

"He hit town six or eight weeks ago. Works sometimes, when he's not on a drunk." The bartender glanced around. "What's he done? Beat the slop out of some jerk?"

"Why do you ask?"

"Big Frank is nuts. Always jumping people."

"For what reason?"

"He don't need a reason. He's just mean."

"Ever seen him with a knife?"

"Yeah. I know he carries one. But I've never seen him pull it on anybody. He's so big he doesn't need to."

"Would you say he's violent?"

"I told you, he's nuts. I've watched him shake down customers for their bread. These guys don't have much money. What, four or five dollars at most? He takes somebody's money, then beats the shit out of him anyway."

"Why don't you just bar him from the joint?" Fred interjected.

"Why don't *you* bar him from the joint?" the bartender shot back.

"In the last two weeks," I said, "have you seen him spend more money than usual?" I wondered if he'd robbed Hines and Robinson.

"No. He's always broke. But then, he don't need much. He shakes down bums for his booze, and what can his food bill be? I tell you, it's weird. He sits here for hours at a time chewing lemons and munching lettuce."

"That's all he eats?"

"All I ever see him eat."

"How about property? Has he tried to sell anything across the bar?"

"No."

"Do you know where Frank lives?"

"No."

"Look," I said, "do me a favor. Keep this conversation to yourself."

"Man, we never talked. This is just a job for me. A lousy one."

"Fred, why *don't* you bar Big Frank from the joint?" I asked on our way to another bar.

He grumbled and kicked some gravel on the sidewalk. "Anybody can act bad, picking on winos."

"Or Hines? Robinson?"

"Yeah. They fall into the same category. One's old. The other's little. Weak."

I flipped the mug shot of Graney at the man selling drinks in the second establishment where we stopped, and he said, distaste and a touch of fear on his face, "Sure, I know Big Frank. But talk to the guy over there." He pointed to a man who looked seventy years old, was probably fifty, white stubbled beard on gnarled, red-splotched drinker's features that took a long, hard lifetime to sculpt. "He's Big Frank's best friend. His only friend. He can tell you all about his buddy."

"Can I buy you a drink, old-timer?" I said.

"I'm not an old-timer. But you can buy me a drink. You're cops, aren't you?"

"And you're a rocket scientist, right?" Dantagnan said.

He looked at Fred with yellowish, bloodshot eyes. "No. But I was a college professor once."

"Look, chief," I said. "We just want to ask you a few questions."

"Questions? What do you want to know from a drunk?"

"I understand you're a friend of Big Frank's."

"He's my partner. What did he do? Wind up in jail again?"

"No. But we've heard complaints about his attitude. Has he got a chip on his shoulder?"

"Most people don't understand Frank. I do. We've traveled the circuit about a year. Apples in Washington, oranges in Florida, lettuce in California. He looks out for me. I translate for him."

"Translate?"

"He has a speech impediment. No education. None at all. Not that a master's degree did me any good. But Frank's hard to understand."

The man emptied his glass of wine. I ordered him another.

"Do you and Frank stay together?"

"Yeah."

"Where?"

"A flophouse on Magazine Street." He gave me the address. "Look, Mister, don't put Frank in jail. He's really harmless. We're heading south, anyway. Florida. I'll calm him down."

"How can you claim he's harmless? Everyone's terrified of him."

"It's his size that frightens people. But I can handle him."

"He mops up the floor with every customer on skid row. Plus, he's taking their money. Doesn't seem you're doing a very good job handling him."

"I can do it. Just give me a chance."

"Have you ever seen blood on Big John's clothes?"

"After he's been fighting."

"What about a knife? Does he carry one?"

The drunk shook his head slowly.

"Does he carry a knife?" I repeated.

"Look, Cap, Big Frank has problems, especially when he's

drunk. But he carries that knife for work. I told you, we pick fruit."

"Let's see *your* knife."

"Cap, I can handle him."

"Does Frank drink in the Quarter?"

"Frank drinks anywhere. Sure, if he's got a few extra bucks, he'll go to the Quarter."

"Where did you and Frank spend Thanksgiving?"

"Thanksgiving? I can't remember where I spent yesterday."

"Did Frank ever—"

"John," Dantagnan interrupted, his eyes slanting across my head to the bar's entrance.

I turned, just an inch or two, and the sight of him filled my vision. He tottered in the doorway like a shabby Paul Bunyan, every part of him big, from feet in size 18 shoes to a huge, flat head from which peered enormous, haughty, confident eyes. Cruel eyes. Big Frank wasn't Paul Bunyan but a king down here, and he knew it. The King of Skid Row. And like kings of yore, he ruled by right of might, no questions tolerated.

The bar took on the eerie silence that precedes a tornado. This tornado in the form of an almost supernaturally large man slowly looked from patron to patron, picking a target.

You don't want to fight this guy, warned my mind urgently. We didn't have probable cause for an arrest, and besides, without benefit of surprise, Fred and I might have to kill him to take him, and that brought honor to no one.

Within an instant of seeing him—he'd already spotted us— Fred and I rose to our feet (we'd talked out this scene years before, like good cop partners should) and headed for the door, trying to appear finished with some routine check. We couldn't arrest him and we didn't dare try to question him.

That would mean reading him his rights, and we wanted heavy-duty ammunition before going that, at best, one-shot route.

My heart pounded and my damn mouth went dry. Four steps ahead stood an ugly scene my partner and I didn't want to play out in a tawdry, filthy theater before a numbed audience. I knew, and so did Fred (he'd been with me at that bloody beginning on Governor Nicholls), that the menacing man we moved toward could be the butcher of gentle William Hines and admirable Rodney Robinson.

Frank knew we were cops. Realizing this, most people perform a deft sidestep maneuver and let us pass. Not Frank. He stood fixed in the open doorway, blotting out the light, bristling with self-assurance and hostility.

We stopped three feet away. "Excuse me," I said.

He didn't move. *Christ Almighty*, I thought.

We couldn't back down. Retreat to where? If a cop does retreat, he loses credibility and stature with his peers (who will surely hear what happened) and, most importantly, his carefully cultivated self–esteem.

Control is essential. Fifteen hundred policemen need to regulate perhaps a million drunks at Mardi Gras, and without firmness the situation quickly deteriorates to chaos. But on this occasion the city—okay, this little piece of it—belonged to Fred and me, so the law held, and we were law *enforcement* officers.

Two seconds passed. It seemed two days.

"Cold outside today," I said.

"Grrrbbl," Frank answered, noncommittally, showing no sign of budging.

Departmental guidelines (often mistakenly called The Book—there is no book) assert that I should now say, "Excuse me, sir, but I need to get through this door. Would you mind stepping aside?" Such an approach was absurd and could only impress Big Frank in a negative way. In reality, I might say, "Look, asshole, I said 'excuse me.' Get the fuck out of the door."

Departmental guidelines, if the subject still doesn't move, advise me to avoid confrontation, perhaps by going to the bar and waiting.

In true life, if the second request was ignored, Fred or I would shove Big Frank hard in the chest, *move him*, get through, and if he wanted more, he himself would make the choice.

Fred, fearing nothing on two legs, preferred the true-life approach. I went to the weather remark, hoping to avoid a bad fight.

"It's going to get a lot hotter if you don't move," I said.

"Grrrbbl." Interrogating Frank, if it came to that, would be a pain.

I didn't take my eyes from this giant—if he detected weakness, we would have a world of trouble—but I could feel Fred, alongside me, breathing heavily, revving himself up, shifting weight from one foot to the other. His patience threshold never registered high, and I knew he'd soon jump on Frank's chest.

Just then this Goliath took a backward step and another to the side. (Who could understand his reason? I didn't think it was a retreat.) Fred and I were by him and out on the sidewalk.

"He only picks on the old and weak, huh?" I said when we reached the car.

"He backed down, didn't he?"

"I don't know. Maybe. But what about when we bring him in for questioning? Tyrone Cole ran. There's no run in Frank."

* * *

I sat rocking a fitfully sleeping Amy in my arms in our living room and listened to Diane tell about the events of her day. The television, the sound turned low, flickered ABC's *Monday Night Football*, a game between the Patriots and the Dolphins.

"I'm glad you're finally home. This afternoon with Amy was very tiring, but I suppose your day's been even rougher."

"What does Dr. Sadler say?"

"He's encouraged by her lowered temperature. She seems to feel better, and she's eating more. You wouldn't believe it now, but she showed some pep earlier. Dr. Sadler hopes the problem was just having her on the wrong medicine."

"Why has it taken her so long to get well? It's only a fever."

"Well, the body uses a fever to overcome infections. Amy's allergic to the penicillin Dr. Sadler prescribed. The new medicine, he thinks, will do the trick. It's a viral infection that knocked her down hard, and it may take a while for her to regain her strength."

"Is the infection contagious?"

"I guess it is."

"Then we have to worry about Todd?"

"No. He would have shown symptoms by now."

I sat and stared unseeing at the football game, with no idea which team was ahead. I couldn't make out the voices of two of the announcers, but Howard Cosell's occasionally came through.

"Tell me about the case," Diane said.

"I'm so tired, honey." True enough, but I also didn't want her worried about any future meeting between me and Big Frank or Crazy Johnny. "I really don't feel like talking about it. I'll catch you up in the morning." After, I thought, figuring how to edit out the more terrifying aspects of their personalities.

"I'm glad you're working with Fred. I feel safer when you're with him."

So did I.

"After you finish this case," Diane said, "why don't you take some time off? We all need it. The family can go somewhere together. Maybe Bea and Fred could join us."

"I'd like to," I began, but Diane raised her hand to shush me.

"Terrible tragedy," I heard, but did not comprehend, Cosell saying.

"Listen," Diane said.

"Some athlete probably sprained his ankle," I said.

"Listen!" Diane got out of her chair and turned the volume up.

"Absolutely shocking," Cosell said, "John Lennon has been shot and killed outside his Central Park West apartment in New York City. Perhaps the most famous of the Beatles, Lennon—"

"Oh, my God," Diane said.

Fully alert, I couldn't think of anything to say.

"So senseless." Tears glistened in my wife's eyes. Diane loved the Beatles, but she'd have reacted this way to anyone's murder.

Surprisingly, I thought about Hines. Robinson. So many others through the years. Then, Lennon again. Suddenly, I was overwhelmed by sadness.

$\equiv$ **11** $\equiv$

John Reilly called Tuesday, December 9, excitement in his voice, and asked me to meet him at Chalmette Battlefield to talk with Benny Burkhart, the owner-operator of a fringe French Quarter neighborhood bar Crazy Johnny frequented. Reilly had tried for days to persuade Burkhart to talk to us but judged the man was too afraid.

I immediately came to the same conclusion upon seeing the nervous club owner. He looked downright scared. Burkhart had refused to meet us at his business establishment, finally choosing instead Chalmette Battlefield, in the New Orleans suburb of the same name, eight miles east of the city, site of the January 1815 Battle of New Orleans.

Tour groups strolled the grounds, reliving the adventures of Andrew Jackson and Jean Lafitte. We stood near several cannons, replicas of weapons used in the decisive battle of the War of 1812.

"Benny," Reilly said, "tell Detective Dillmann what you know about Johnny."

I lifted my eyes from the patch of grass I was staring at, looked at Burkhart, and waited.

His face—pale from nocturnal workdays—twitched, and I

could almost read the second thoughts he harbored about this meeting. He looked at the grass, opened his mouth, tried to speak, but no sound crossed his trembling lips.

Someone or something had made a big impression on Benny Burkhart.

"Benny," I said, "I can tell you're shook. From what I've heard about Johnny, you probably should be. But remember, we're meeting way out here to keep your involvement private. You know John Reilly, and I'm sure you trust him. Believe me, I'll also keep anything you tell me in strictest confidence. It won't leave this field."

"Detective Dillmann," he said, finding the words with difficulty, "they don't call him Crazy Johnny for nothing. If he knew I was talking with you, I'd be in deep shit. He carries this Buck knife, you know."

I didn't know. I looked at Reilly's smug smile. He'd informed me—call it intuition—from almost the beginning that Crazy Johnny was our killer.

"Have you actually seen this knife?"

"Seen it? I held it in my safe the whole month of August."

Had this been the murder weapon?

"When you say Buck knife, is that a brand name, or a type of knife?"

"It's a brand of hunting knife. Wooden handle. Six-inch blade."

Burkhart was going okay now, and I wanted to keep him talking before the second thoughts returned.

"Can you remember when you gave the knife back to him?"

"Not exactly. You see, Johnny used to drink in my place. He was always in trouble, always fighting. Early in August, he got in a fight on the banquette in front of the bar. Somebody called the cops. Johnny ran in, handed me the knife, and asked me to hide it. He didn't want to get picked up carrying a concealed weapon."

"Why did you hold it so long?"

"Stupidity, I guess. But you'd have to meet Johnny to know what I'm talking about. To look at him, most of the time you'd think he's a choirboy, the kid next door. I didn't want to see him get in trouble. I knew he had a temper and feared he'd stab someone when he got into a drunken rage. But that was the funny part. When he looked mad, like he wanted to torch the whole city, that's when he was nice."

"I don't understand. What do you mean?"

"He'd sit on a bar stool, steaming, and actually seem to grow in size. He'd mutter. Curse. Pound his fists. I'd ask him, What is it? and he'd say in a loud threatening voice, 'I love you, Benny! I love the whole beautiful world!' It took a while, but I learned he was sincere. When he swore and carried on, he said the nicest things. He meant them. He'd do things, volunteer to help. When he looked nice, that's when you had to watch out."

"Tell me about the 'nice' times."

"Real horror shows. And, Jesus, looking back, I think maybe I dreamed them. But I didn't. Johnny would sit on that bar stool, clean shaven, smiling sweetly. He has the smile of an innocent child, almost angelic. He's such a good-looking young man when he wants to be. I swear, Detective Dillmann, you could almost see a halo over his head at times like this. A customer would walk in, look the bar up and down, and choose the seat next to Johnny. Who could resist? Johnny would smile at him just right. 'Hey,' the look said, 'you want some friendly conversation? A sympathetic ear? Sit down right here.' The guy would. Before he had time to call out a drink order, Johnny would be in his face, nose to nose with the guy, that angel smile all over his face, and he'd speak in the most unfriendly way. He'd say, 'You're an idiot. You serve no purpose in the world, yet you breathe my air.' The customer had maybe a thousandth of a second to figure things out, nowhere enough time, before

— 163 —

Johnny would shove him off his stool onto the floor, leap on
him, and start kicking ass. I mean this dickens can fight. He
doesn't look it, but he's five ten, one hundred and eighty-five
pounds of tight muscle that becomes absolutely frenzied. I saw
this happen three, four times, and it scared the hell out of me.
He'd be smiling real nice and pounding the shit out of someone.
Even his eyes smiled. They weren't cold or mean, like someone
might have with a glued-on expression. No, all of him smiled.''
  The last look Hines and Robinson saw?
  "Benny," I said, "if this asshole's so frightening, why did
you give back the knife?"
  "I didn't want to, but look at it from my side. He was bad
for business, and he kept coming around, asking for that damn
blade. I knew better, but what choice did I have? I finally
gave it to him across the bar.''
  "Did he say anything?"
  "Just smiled." Burkhart thought about this for a moment.
"Detective Dillmann, you're sure Johnny won't find out about
this meeting? This guy's not bullshit. He'd come after me.
Some of my customers say he's still in the Quarter and crazy
as ever. I don't want him around my place.''
  "Benny, I can't pick Johnny up for being crazy or because
he carries a Buck knife. We'd have to haul in hundreds just
like him. Relax. There's no reason for him to find out, and
if it comes to a trial, I don't think we need your testimony.''
  "Thank God for that.''
  "Benny, you seem pretty well acquainted with Johnny.
Don't you know his last name?"
  "He calls himself John Lloyd, but I don't think that's it.''
  "Reach way down to answer this next question. Did you
ever have a customer named Bill Hines?"
  "The name doesn't ring a bell." Burkhart looked thought-
ful. "Wasn't he the man killed a couple of weeks ago? You
think Johnny did it?"

"I don't know. What do you think?"

"He's damn sure capable."

"Do you know anything else about him? Where he's from? Where he's worked? His family? Anything at all that can help?"

"Unfortunately, no. He doesn't talk much about himself. He gets whacked out on dust, you know. Angel dust."

Craig Masters, investment banker, worked out of One Shell Square, a new fifty-story-plus office building on Poydras Street in the heart of the city's business district. Reilly and I got to his office at 2:10 P.M., at his request, since, he explained, the New York Stock Exchange closed at three o'clock EST.

Masters's office, plush and modern, furnished a fine view of the Mississippi River, gray and swiftly flowing. Masters himself, twenty-eight, six feet tall, athletically built, tanned to last the winter, wore a three-piece gray business suit, button-down collar, and conservative tie. A young businessman in the fast lane. He shook hands firmly with Reilly and me, motioned us to sit, resumed his position in his leather executive chair, and looked at his watch.

"What can I do for you gentlemen?"

"Mr. Masters," I said, "I understand you were involved in an altercation at Kelly's Corner bar a few months back."

"Yes, unfortunately I was."

"Do you recall the name of the man you fought with?"

"Sure. I'll never forget him or his name. It's John Floyd."

"Are you sure it isn't Lloyd?"

"Positive. It was Floyd with an *F*. What's this all about?"

"We're trying to locate Floyd."

"What did he do?"

"We want to question him about some cases. Mr. Masters, I'd like to hear what happened between you and Floyd."

"I'd rather just forget it. I can't believe animals like Floyd exist."

"What happened?"

"On my way home from playing tennis with some clients at City Park, I was overheated and thirsty, so I stopped at Kelly's to get a cold one. This is unbelievable. I go into the bar, order my beer, and this Floyd character walks up to me, smiles, and asks where I bought the cute tennis shorts. I thought he was kidding. I'm six feet. In good shape. Why would this jerk pick a fight with me? I laughed and blew him off, figuring I'd get my beer and leave. But he kept it up. He tells me only faggots wear shorts. I asked, 'What in the hell's your problem?' The next thing I know, he's swinging on me. Just like that, for no reason. Well, I figured I'd whip his ass. He sure deserved it. But this guy was either crazy or on something, because my punches didn't faze him. A couple of customers pulled us apart, but they couldn't hold him. He broke away and started slugging me again while I was being held. They turned me loose and three of us grabbed Floyd and tried to hold him down, but it was impossible. You wouldn't believe this punk's strength for his size. Like I said, he had to be on something. Anyway, when the cops got there, the only way they could calm him was by threatening to use their nightsticks."

"Did they arrest him?"

"Damn right. But to show you how crazy this bozo is, he was laughing. I mean, laughing out loud, even after the police handcuffed him and put him in the back of the squad car. The oddest thing of all, it wasn't a nasty or insane laugh. More like someone having fun, or laughing at a good joke."

"What happened when you went to court? Was he convicted?"

"Well, I'm ashamed to say this, but I'd flown to New York on business and couldn't get back for the trial. I guess they let him go."

* * *

With Reilly looking over my shoulder, I entered John Floyd into the NCIC computer in the homicide office. Within seconds, his name and arrest record glowed on the screen:

4-12-75 Refusal to pay food bill

6-19-77 Disturbing the peace (fighting)

6-26-77 Obstructing a public place (refusing to leave a bar as instructed)

8-15-79 Felony possession (over $500) of stolen property

8-16-79 Possession of narcotics

For some reason, the early August battery arrest wasn't listed.

The computer gave the blond-haired, blue-eyed Floyd's birthday as 6-29-49 and listed his occupation as engineer. I doubted he was any sort of engineer I'd ever heard of. The computer noted a Minden, Louisiana, address, probably outdated. The machine, if you knew how to read it, described him as a violent, drug-abusing thief.

I'd pulled records far worse than the thirty-one-year-old Floyd's, though. Often, before a perpetrator graduates to murder, his penchant for violence manifests itself much more dramatically; aggravated rape for example, or assault with intent to kill.

On the other hand, who could say John Floyd hadn't tried to kill during those fights? The ferocity he brought to these battles harked back to a different age.

Carrying a mug shot of our suspect and five fill-in photos (B of I pictures resembling him), I went to Gerald Griffin's home and counted myself lucky to find the oil worker there.

I spread the photos in front of him, and when he immediately identified John Floyd as the man he'd escorted to Charity Hospital, I asked him to look more closely. "You need to be sure. Absolutely sure."

"There's no doubt in my mind," he said. "That's definitely him."

Back at my desk, I tried to shut out the surrounding hubbub and mentally review where I stood. I didn't have enough probable cause to pick up Big Frank and the Crazy Johnny situation was iffy.

The investigation demanded that I focus more on Floyd. Even though both violent men carried knives and came highly recommended as the perpetrator (Big Frank by Hollis, Crazy Johnny by Reilly), it was evident that Floyd had gone out of his way to convince Gerald Griffin that he (Floyd) should not be held responsible for his actions.

A big question: Was Crazy Johnny crazy? Could an individual cunning enough to orchestrate a defense prior to his arrest have wreaked the violence and destruction I'd seen at the Hines murder?

What did I really have on Graney? Bloody trousers—a thousand explanations for this—and Hollis's word for his guilt. Hollis would never testify.

What did I have on Floyd? One, he hid a knife, unfortunately before the killings, not after, in an attempt to conceal damaging evidence. Two, he mentioned the Fairmont murder to Gerald Griffin on the way to Charity Detox Center. Three, he showed concern about establishing himself as not responsible for his actions while on drugs during his walk with the Good Samaritan.

In other words, almost zip on both Big Frank and Crazy Johnny. I'd fizzled out with Cole, and I wanted strong cards in my hand the next time I went for a confession, which was this case's most likely solution.

My plans for Big Frank: I'd ask bartenders in the Warehouse District to call me the moment Frank came in with a knife, and I'd have First District uniforms pick him up. They'd charge him with carrying a concealed weapon. Once the knife was confiscated and in our possession, lab tests could determine if the weapon had been used in the murders. Positive test results wouldn't give me sufficient evidence for an arrest warrant, but would establish enough probable cause to question him.

My plans for Crazy Johnny: In a word, Reilly. The beat cop believed bone-deep in Floyd's guilt, and I could count on his utterly tireless pursuit of the puzzle's missing pieces.

What if neither Frank Graney nor John Floyd panned out? On heater cases, all the detectives in NOPD Homicide keep themselves updated, speculate over beers at the Miracle Mile, form theories, and offer suggestions for the investigating detective. Most, but not all, of these experts who deal in death daily believed a black man killed Rodney Robinson. Their opinions deserved respect, and Mike Rice devoted his energies and expertise to the black-murderer angle.

Rice and I, the two closest to the investigation, believed we dealt with a single killer. But we'd keep an open mind and go where the evidence pointed.

Mike interviewed Nedra Boykin again—he too had doubts about her—dug deep into his bag of black informants, and cast out every conceivable net to snare our killer. The same things I'd have done if I'd handled both murders.

We each did what we had to, kept the other informed, and hoped to share the victory of cracking the case.

12

Our elephantine efforts didn't produce even a mouse until December 15, six days after the interviews with Burkhart and Masters. Credit for the breakthrough again went to Reilly.

His call came at midnight while I slept. I had somehow trained myself to pick up the phone fast so Diane wouldn't be awakened—sometimes it worked, other times it didn't—but this night my hand brushed hers on the way to the receiver. She sat up, wide awake and disapproving. Amy's troubles had at last been traced to the penicillin allergy—she was getting better slowly—and our life together had returned to as close to normal as it would ever get. Diane knew that ringing phone meant trouble.

"John, this is John Reilly."

"Yeah, John. What you got?"

"Floyd's our boy. I knew it."

"Are you sure?"

"I got a witness."

The magic word *witness* woke me up like a bucket of ice water splashed over my head.

"A witness to the murder?"

"No. He didn't see it. But he talked to Floyd. Look, John, it's a long story. Do you want me to take a statement?"

"No. Don't do anything. Where are you?"

"In the Quarter at the Mississippi River Bottom bar on St. Philip Street."

"Wait for me. I'll see you in about an hour. Hold that witness, John. Cuff him if you have to."

I looked at Diane, knowing what would come.

"Don't tell me you have to go back to work tonight," she said. "This is ridiculous."

"Di," I said weakly, "this is what I've been waiting for. We might have the case broke."

"Do you have to go now?"

"Of course I do. You heard the call."

"Are you coming back home, or will you work right through?"

"You ask me that all the time. I don't know. I'll call you, honey."

"Okay," she said, not a happy cell in her body. She rolled over, pulled up the blanket, and feigned sleep. But then she couldn't resist: "Anybody going to be with you?"

"John Reilly. He's there."

"Well, be careful."

I drove our 1977 Caprice over the twin spans, Interstate 10, built across Lake Pontchartrain, doing eighty-five miles per hour, a hot cup of 7-Eleven coffee in my hand. A good, but too often abused, thing about being a cop is knowing you'll *never* get a speeding ticket.

Reilly sat at a corner table in the big bar next to a man I judged to be forty, dressed in slacks and open shirt, seeming relaxed. I learned quickly why Reilly didn't need to cuff him.

"John Dillmann," Reilly said, "meet Steven Edwards. Steve owns this bar. Steve, meet Detective Dillmann."

"I understand you're Homicide."

"Yes. I imagine John told you I'm handling the Bill Hines investigation."

"I knew Bill. He was a good, gentle man."

"How long have you known Crazy Johnny?"

"Two years. I own several places in the Quarter, and Johnny's barred from all of them."

I'd thought him relaxed? Close up, Edwards looked so edgy I feared he might bolt from his own saloon.

"Fighting, right?"

"You got it. When Johnny gets liquored up, he's wacko."

"Bad as everyone says?"

"I've seen him in maybe a dozen fights. The man's dangerous." Second, third, even fourth thoughts registered on Edwards's face.

"What do you know about the Hines murder?" Maybe I could get him through it.

"Look, Detective Dillmann, I've got something to say first, off the record."

"Shoot."

"I've known John Reilly for years. I trust him. He says I can trust you, or I wouldn't be talking to you now. This motherfucker Floyd's a psycho, and I'm in the Quarter all hours of the night. If he knows I've talked to you, he'll put that shiv in me first. I need your guarantee to keep me out of this."

"Steve, I can't make that kind of guarantee. But I can promise you this: If Johnny killed Bill Hines and I bust him, he'll stay in jail. He can't hurt you from there. And another thing: You told me you knew Bill Hines and he was a good man. I was in his apartment. I looked at his blood-covered body. If Crazy Johnny was responsible for that, we better all forget about guarantees and work toward getting him off the street. Now, please, tell me what you know." We eyed each other a moment.

"Several days after Bill's murder—in fact, I'd just read about the killing—on my way to work, I saw Johnny on the sidewalk, about to stagger into my place. I could tell he was really fucked up. I yelled at him, 'Johnny, you can't go in there!' When I reached the entrance I said, 'You always cause problems. You're barred. So beat it!' That's when he said, 'You better quit fucking with me. I already wasted one person.' I said, 'Who? Bill Hines?' I'd just read the newspaper story. He said, 'Yeah, on Governor Nicholls.' I was scared and yelled, 'I don't give a shit! Get away from here!' He smiled and staggered off down the street."

"Steve, this is very important. Are you positive, absolutely positive, that he, not you, mentioned Governor Nicholls?"

"He did. I'm sure."

"Did Bill Hines frequent your bar?"

"He came in occasionally."

"Think back. Have you ever seen Hines in the company of Crazy Johnny?"

"Not that I recall. Anyway, Bill wouldn't associate with that nut. Johnny's brutal and violent. Bill wouldn't have gone near him."

But Johnny wasn't always brutal and violent. He could don the face of an angel.

"During all those fights, did you ever see Johnny with a knife?"

"No. Never."

"Why did you wait more than two weeks to reveal this information?"

"I guess I'm as bad as everybody else. I don't want trouble in my place. I'm afraid for my own safety. What can I say?"

"You can identify Johnny from a photo, can't you?"

"No problem."

"I'll need you to come down to my office, look at some pictures, and give me a statement."

"Now?"

"Now."

Steven Edwards gave his statement, just as he related it in the Mississippi River Bottom bar, and scored again for our side by easily picking John Floyd's picture from a tough photo lineup.

Rice was working graveyard this morning. After making sure Edwards got back to his business via the best service NOPD could provide (a uniform car), I told Mike the latest.

"Beans," I said, "good news!"

"Must be, for you to be here at this godawful hour."

"It's Crazy Johnny. At least on Hines."

"You got him, right?"

"No, I haven't brought him in yet. But he's running his mouth about Hines. He's given us enough to pick him up."

"What about Robinson? Is Johnny my man too?"

"Same killer, Mike. I'm still betting on it."

"Christ, don't pick him up without me."

"I can't promise, but I'll try to give you a pisser call." A call made at a bad time: for me, the middle of the night; for him, the middle of the day.

Time to shake John Floyd out of the Quarter. He told Edwards he had killed Hines. Adding spice, he referred to the murder by location, not the victim's name (the type of deranged jargon typical of a perpetrator).

Finding Johnny should be easy, or so I thought. He had a high profile, regular watering holes, and no one likely to shelter him for long. Already this December 15 I began imagining my one-on-one with Crazy Johnny in London's office.

Reilly had come with me to Homicide for Steven Edwards's statement. That accomplished, I dispatched John back to the Quarter with encouragement and urgings (all unnecessary—he too sensed the end and wanted it almost as much as breath) to find Floyd and contact me immediately. I hoped Rice could make the arrest with us.

But Reilly didn't call all morning. When he did, in the early afternoon, he said, "Jesus Christ, John, I can't believe it. He's vanished. No one's seen him."

"Think he's left town?"

"Could be. But he's felt no heat from us."

"Maybe someone in the bar saw us talking to Edwards and passed the word."

"Johnny doesn't have a friend that good."

"Get some rest, Reilly. Pick it up again tonight."

That night, the next night, and the next, no Crazy Johnny. London fumed. I lived and relived that interrogation scene with Johnny, even in my dreams, but it didn't materialize.

We did locate a few individuals who had heard Crazy Johnny bragging about "drilling holes" in the heads of several people when he worked oil rigs offshore—information that my brain assimilated uncomfortably.

Once we punctured the dam of silence, we were flooded with stories about Floyd's activities. Account after dreary account portrayed a Dr. Jekyll/Mr. Hyde brawler apparently bent on nothing short of killing during his unprovoked attacks. Only outside intervention halted the murderous assaults. Johnny never stopped himself, even with a victim nearly unconscious.

During these interviews, I began to develop my own idea of how the killings came down. Hines, a lonely man, and Robinson, ever gregarious and good-hearted ("Maybe he picked up a hitchhiker," his friend David Hennessey said), may have run into Johnny, thought him a decent person down on his luck, taken pity, and offered him a place to crash for the night. It happens more often than people think, an individual temporarily sheltering a stranger. Not exactly a

Looking for Mr. Goodbar scenario, but analogous, and, like giving a hitchhiker a ride, potentially very dangerous.

The Hines/Robinson murders occupied front-and-center space in my mind. But our inability to find Floyd and the senselessness of spinning our wheels (a stakeout at Louisiana Purchase, for example, when we knew the bartender would call the moment he spotted Johnny), allowed me time to clean up several cases.

Still, I did odd things, indicators of my real priorities. I researched the first name of "Pretty Boy" Floyd, the gangster that Melvin Purvis and a band of federal agents killed in 1934 in an Ohio field. For some reason I thought Pretty Boy's first name had been John, the same as our Floyd, but it was Charles.

I looked up "Baby Face" Nelson, killed by federal agents in Chicago a month after Pretty Boy Floyd bought the farm.

Baby Face and Pretty Boy. Maybe their lives could furnish insight into the man with the Eagle Scout looks I searched for. Nothing. Nelson had been just a fairly decent-looking thug, perhaps less depraved than our pretty boy, a thin veneer of "class" attached to him—largely by the press—but, at bottom, a killer.

John Floyd's looks, like the handsome appeal of mass-murderer Ted Bundy, worked in his favor. If he'd been intimidating, like Big Frank, potential victims could have recognized the menace and steered clear. Bundy trapped young women with charm and promises of modeling careers; I suspected Crazy Johnny lured with honey and pathetic, endearing pleas for help.

The more I thought—and I had to watch this, keep my mind open—the more Big Frank faded from the picture. I suspected, but couldn't prove, that security at the Fairmont was preoccupied or sidetracked at the time Robinson led his killer into the lobby. Two nice-looking young men might not be noticed, even by guests. A lumbering Herman Munster with the ferocious appearance of Big Frank Graney couldn't be missed.

Frank seemed extremely unlikely paired with Hines, also. No forced entry at the victim's apartment meant Hines *admitted* the killer, and I couldn't imagine that happening with Graney.

When Christmas came (tough horse-trading with other detectives—I had to give up three holidays to get the day off), I vowed not to let Johnny ruin it for my family, and I mostly succeeded.

Once she knew I'd be free, Diane topped her usual yuletide decorating blitz. She placed luminaries up the path from the sidewalk to our front door, added new, handmade ornaments to the tall tree reaching toward the cathedral ceiling in the living room, and baked a delicious assortment of confections that made us all forget our waistlines.

On Christmas morning Amy, back to her old chipper self, squealed with excitement at the sight of her shiny Huffy bike with butterflies on the banana seat (once again it fell to Diane's lot to assemble the toys while I worked my security job), and Todd challenged me to a game on his new Electronic Battleship.

Diane noticed a little black nose sniffing and claws scratching at airholes in her present from me. When she opened the box, a ball of white Himalayan fluff wearing a big red ribbon jumped out. She named the kitten Chrystabelle from a poem she'd read, and we all learned it quickly by making repeated demands on the scampering feline to quit snagging upholstered furniture and climbing drapes.

Diane's sister Linda and her husband, Don Guillot, spent the night on Christmas Eve, and the house filled with other relatives for Christmas dinner in the early afternoon.

All in all, a wonderful Christmas, and before the New Year was rung in, a break in the case: another witness against Crazy Johnny. On December 30, I talked with Gene Reed, fifty-eight years old, a bindery worker with O'Donnell Brothers Printing and Office Supplies. The day before, the twenty-ninth, Floyd, who knew Reed, walked up to the bindery worker on the street: "Johnny was feeling very good. He wanted money. When I refused to give him some, he said, 'I'll take care of you, like I did the one at the Fairmont.'"

Reed's information helped. Floyd had now linked himself with *both* murders, each time referring to them by location. It seemed entirely possible he never knew, or had forgotten, the names of his victims. To him they had become Governor Nicholls and the Fairmont Hotel.

All that remained was finding Johnny and trying to break him. Clichés cluttered my mind when I thought of attempting to obtain his confession: we did or we didn't; make or break; all or nothing. Rice called it "the Super Bowl."

Latin provided the correct phrase: *sine qua non.*

Our frustration was almost explosive. Johnny was in the Quarter, a one square mile area; at least Reed had seen him there on the twenty-ninth of December and despite all legal efforts (we didn't have enough evidence to put out a Wanted), we couldn't find him. Every informant in the Quarter knew we were searching for him and would be grateful to the individual who turned him, but they weren't running a race to police headquarters to snitch.

Each day I drove into the Quarter and cruised his haunts, watching for him on the street, peering into the joints where he drank. This wasn't the way to succeed, and I knew it. The scenario that figured was the one that came down.

"It's D-Day. Floyd's moving." On January 19, 1981, I met Reilly in the restaurant of the Bourbon Orleans. The old-fashioned beat cop, one of perhaps a thousand sets of eyes looking for Johnny, came through.

"I got a call from one of my people this morning," Reilly said. "Floyd's on the street."

"Good work. We'll pick him up."

Reilly was ready. He sprang to his feet, and I had to motion him to sit back down.

"Reilly, we need a game plan. I don't want to go off half-cocked." But I wanted to *go.* Adrenaline was already pumping, too soon—and now with the end in sight I had to sit a little longer. The arrest didn't promise to be easy, and we needed every advantage. A plan would be a big help. Even Fred and I, who knew each other's moves backward and forward, planned whenever we had the luxury.

"How do you want to take him?" Reilly said.

"As easily as possible. He's still just a suspect."

Reilly sneered for both of us.

"We see him on the street," I said, "there's no problem. Short and sweet. I'll jack him"—shove him against a wall—"and you frisk and cuff him. If he's in a bar, things could get hairy. We don't want customers hurt."

Reilly removed a blackjack from his back pocket and placed it on the table. "If the asshole fights, this will calm him down."

But maybe not. I thought about PCP.

"You talk to him first," I said. "Put him at ease. I'll do the talking when we take him, and you watch his hands. Watch him close. We'll try and get him outside or near the door, anywhere away from the customers. Once he's clear, we'll grab him."

"I'm ready. Let's go."

"Reilly, remember, watch his hands. If he moves toward his pocket, or swings at me, lay it on him. I want this over quick."

We faced the worst kind of arrest. Floyd used drugs, including PCP. He was a proven fighter, credited with unnatural strength. And I believed he'd committed two vicious murders.

The "I believed" is what made it tough. If we had eyewitnesses or reliable physical evidence, or even enough for an arrest warrant, I'd stick a gun in his face, no more planning needed. But he was only a suspect; this wasn't an arrest. A difficult situation, but our safety came first.

We started at The Pub, a hangout for locals. No Johnny. We went across the street to Le Bistro. No Johnny. We headed toward Rampart Street and the Louisiana Purchase bar, several blocks away.

I felt excited, apprehensive, and scared. Excited because the solution might have finally arrived. Apprehensive because a thousand things could easily go wrong. And scared of the pain of being cut, of sharp steel tearing my flesh. Reilly ranked as a reliable partner in this situation, but I knew I'd feel safer with Fred or Mike Rice. I'd survived dangerous encounters with both of them before.

I saw John Floyd for the first time through the open door of the Louisiana Purchase. He was my weight and an inch shorter. Somehow I'd pictured a much bigger man. I had been told about but wasn't prepared for his All-American good looks. His hair was more blond and his eyes more blue than I'd expected; a handsome young man I could imagine on the tennis court with Masters, rather than rolling around with him on a barroom floor. He wore a clean shirt and pressed slacks.

Reilly and I stepped inside the bar, our eyes glued to Johnny, who was propped on a barstool. Unbidden, my mind clicked to a shot of the Hines murder scene. I moved a step closer, Reilly alongside. And although at first Mr. Clean-Cut seemed not to belong in that Governor Nicholls snapshot, my mind clicked to another picture, and there he was.

We came nearer. Johnny didn't notice. He looked at peace with the world, a model of serenity, a good, approachable kid—thirty-one, but younger in appearance—who wouldn't harm a fly. I knew on good authority that he was now at his most dangerous.

Reilly took the stool to Johnny's right, placing himself between Floyd and the door, and I sat on Reilly's right. Floyd would have to get by both of us if he made for the door, a choice that would delight us. We'd follow him and not have to worry about the Purchase's fifteen or so customers. I ordered a beer, Reilly a cocktail.

Ostensibly I looked at Reilly, but actually beyond him to our suspect. Johnny still hadn't taken notice of us. He wore a contented smile, as if contemplating some pleasant memory from a happy childhood. All my "go" systems registered ready.

"Let me buy you a beer," Reilly said to Johnny after several minutes, when it became clear our suspect intended to stay for the duration.

"Sure," Floyd said, gratitude adding itself to his pleasing countenance.

Reilly turned his back to me and started making small talk. I could never have pulled it off, but my new partner had a rap for everybody who lived on his beat. He wanted Johnny relaxed and in a cooperative mood when we asked him to take a ride with us to headquarters.

I watched a half hour of this. Johnny smiled all the time, normally a good sign, but not in this situation. I found myself both repulsed and entranced by his performance, if such it was. Repulsed because I felt sure I'd seen his handiwork; entranced, against my will, by a come-hither charm that almost glowed. I shook myself, driven by the impulse to get it over with; we couldn't spend the day drinking with him.

I tapped Reilly on the back. He swiveled his head a bit sideways, and I whispered, "It's time."

I stood up, walked around Reilly, and stationed myself, heart pounding, on the other side of Floyd. We had him sandwiched. He took notice of *that*, wheeled on his stool, and looked at me with the friendliest eyes I'd later hope never to see again.

"You're John Floyd, aren't you?" I said.

"Yeah. How do you know?" The smile never changed. Nothing changed. If he suspected something bad was about to happen, nothing gave it away.

"John Reilly and I are police officers. We want to talk to you."

Floyd and I had dead eye-contact. I prayed that Reilly, as instructed, watched Johnny's hands, because I expected a frenzy any minute.

"Talk about what?"

"Talk about the decision you have to make." I never looked away from his eyes. He never released mine. His were happy eyes; mine burned with the memory of what I had seen that terrible afternoon on Governor Nicholls.

Floyd laughed pleasantly. "What decision? I don't know what the fuck you're talking about."

I raised my voice an octave. "You and I are going downtown to my office."

"Man, I'm not going anywhere."

"That's where your decision comes in."

"What in hell *are* you talking about?"

"Isn't your nickname 'Crazy'? Crazy Johnny?"

"Yeah, so?"

"So, you can walk out of here cool, or you can live up to

that name. But if you even breathe hard, Reilly and I are going to beat you half to death. Now, how crazy are you? It's up to you."

The smile—Huckleberry Finn wore that smile!—stayed right in place. *Here we go*, I thought. This is what Hines and Robinson saw before the storm broke: a pretty smile and friendly eyes. What all those people he fought with saw. It was going to be awful, going against someone with a drug-induced tolerance for pain.

Those unforgettable eyes bore straight through mine to the back of my skull; not the slightest glint in his eyes betrayed him.

Reilly had come to his feet, hulking over Floyd, a cobra poised to strike.

Floyd shrugged. "Let's go," he said, and started to get up. I shoved him back down on the stool. "Reilly," I said, "you walk out first. Floyd, you follow Officer Reilly. Walk slow. Remember, I'll be right behind you."

Roles reversed with our positions; everything Reilly had done I now had to do. *Watch his hands,* I reminded myself, *watch closely. Any movement at all, jump him.*

The twenty feet to the door seemed the length of a football field. We were a strange procession, and I wondered if it would really be this easy. Not for Floyd it wouldn't be.

The moment Reilly hit the sidewalk, he turned to face our suspect as I grabbed a handful of his hair with my left hand and the collar of his shirt with my right. I slammed him into the front of the building, keeping him disabled by yanking back on his head and neck.

Reilly pulled both of Floyd's wrists behind his back into handcuffs. I frisked him, made him sit on the sidewalk, and waited while Reilly went for the police car.

When we turned him around and sat him down, I advised him of his rights, not really looking at him as I did. When I asked if he understood, he still had that smile that could charm the devil himself, and this after some pretty abrupt treatment.

We put Johnny in a detective-bureau holding cell, and gave him some time to think. I didn't want to rush him and give a defense attorney the opening to say we'd brought in, flustered, and frightened his client into a confession, all while the poor man's head spun.

Flustered? Johnny looked relaxed enough to star in a Beautyrest mattress commercial. *I* was the anxious one.

I gave him three full hours. It dragged by like three days. I passed time going over in my head for the hundredth time the best way to handle the interrogation. If Floyd didn't confess, the deaths of Hines and Robinson almost surely would go unpunished.

=13=

I faced Floyd across Steve London's desk, having already telephoned Mike Rice. He deserved to take the Rodney Robinson confession, if it got that far. But I wasn't sure I could get beyond the smile Floyd fixed on me.

Again I advised Crazy Johnny of his rights, knowing Reilly paced outside the door, prepared to play soft cop, with me in the unaccustomed role of hard nose. If we reached the right point, with Floyd needing a sympathetic shoulder to lean on, Reilly would know the right buttons to push.

"Floyd," I began. "Johnny" seemed too friendly. "You've been mouthing off in the Quarter about killing people. Why don't you tell me about it?"

The smile and eyes radiated innocence. Whoever said eyes are the windows of the soul never met this man.

"I haven't said anything like that. You've got the wrong person."

"Bullshit!" I snapped, hoping this aggressive tack would work. I held up his B of I photo and said, "You know who this is?"

He didn't answer. I thought about Hines and Robinson and wanted to slap the smile right off his face.

I yelled at him. "You know who this is?"

"Yes. It's me."

I turned the picture around, holding it away from him. "These names on the back are witnesses who have fingered you, John Floyd. You've barhopped your way through the French Quarter saying you murdered this person and that person, running your mouth bragging about it. Is that what you think, Floyd? That killing people makes you a big man?"

No answer.

I stood up from the chair, filling the room with my voice. "I asked you, do you think you're a big man?"

He lowered his head, a good sign. Tyrone Cole *lifted* his, because he wasn't a bit worried.

Floyd's head came up slowly. He'd turned into something angry and snarling, the metamorphosis so sudden and complete it startled me.

"I didn't kill anybody!" he spat. "Maybe I did brag. You're right. I was just acting like a big shot. But I didn't really do it."

I expected foam to bubble out of his mouth—he wore the wild look that people expect from their killers.

"Convince me, Floyd. Convince me you didn't kill these people. Think about it. I'm gonna get coffee; when I come back in here, I want you to convince me you're not a murderer."

"How's it going?" Reilly lit on me the instant I closed the door.

"It's going."

I felt an audience of eyes as detectives peered at me from their desks in the gray, chaotic room, asking silent questions about the "something big" brewing in the Division's current heater case. I'd watched from their vantage point plenty of times.

"What's he say?" Reilly pressed.

"That he was just playing Mr. Big Shot and didn't kill anybody."

"Bullshit! He snuffed 'em both."

I thought so. I fetched a cup of coffee and returned to London's office, slammed the door hard, resumed my seat, and cocked both feet up on the desk. "All right, Mr. Floyd, I'm listening."

He looked at me through eyes starting to tear. "Can we talk? Can we really talk?"

A multiple-personality? The three faces of Floyd? Maybe I could understand this third one. I had no clue about the first two.

"Yeah, Johnny, we can talk. Just stop the bullshit and level with me."

"I need help. If I tell you the truth, will you help me?"

"What kind of help do you need?"

"I'm not responsible for what I do. I've got problems. Big problems."

I wanted to give him one he could feel: my hands squeezing his throat. I knew he'd tuned up to sing the same sad song he used on Griffin.

"What kinds of problems?"

"Whiskey. Drugs. I need help."

"Are you telling me you're not responsible for killing two people because you were drunk? You want me to buy that?"

His face contorted, the tears evaporated. He screamed, "I didn't kill anybody! Can't you understand? I'm all talk! I might say anything when I'm in that condition!"

Everyone in the homicide room heard his shouts, but I knew no one would come to check.

"Settle down, Floyd. Tell me about yourself. Have you ever been married?"

"Yeah, a long time ago."

"Do you have any children?"

"Two. They're twelve and nine, I think."

"Where are you living now?"

"In the Quarter. Mostly I stay with friends."

He had friends?

JOHN DILLMANN

"Where were you born?"

"Mississippi, a little place in Mississippi."

"How much education do you have?"

"Sixth grade."

"Can you read and write?"

"A little. Enough to get by."

"You said you drink a lot?"

"Yeah. Mostly whiskey. That's how I got hung with the name Crazy."

"Are you on drugs now?"

"No."

"When did you last take something?"

"This morning."

"What drugs do you use?"

"Anything. Mostly angel dust. That's about all I can afford."

"Were you on drugs when you killed Bill Hines?"

The angel's smile graced his countenance.

"Yeah, I killed him. And the guy at the Fairmont, too. They didn't deserve to live."

He said the magic words. But his conversational, everyday tone shook me. I got up, opened the door, and asked Reilly to come in. The big cop seated himself next to Johnny.

"Floyd, tell Officer Reilly what you just told me."

"I need help. I've been using drugs and drinking too much. I don't remember half the things I say. Detective Dillmann said y'all would help me."

"Tell him what else you said."

"About what?"

I stood up again. "Goddammit, Floyd, quit fucking around! Didn't you tell me you killed Hines and the tourist at the Fairmont?"

His face twisted in hate. "You fucking liar! I *told* you! I didn't kill anybody! I need help! You said you'd help me!"

— 190 —

"Reilly, talk to this crazy motherfucker. I don't want to look at him anymore."

I stormed out, almost knocking down Mike Rice. He'd arrived for the climax, eagerness written all over his face. I suspected he'd been listening at the door.

"How's it going?" Rice asked. "Did he break?"

"Not yet. Mike, I'm telling you, he's guilty as sin. He's trying to con me like he conned Griffin."

"What do you mean?"

"He confessed to me."

"On Robinson too?"

"Yeah. But as soon as Reilly came in, he denied it. He's putting on his Crazy show. Keeps saying he's not responsible because of the drugs and alcohol, and needs help. I'll tell you this, Beans, he's our man. I'm sure."

"Let me try."

"Not yet. Reilly's with him."

"Reilly!"

"It's okay. He's calming Johnny down."

"All right. I have a daily to type. Holler when you're ready for me."

"I'll call you before we get deep into Robinson. You should take that confession."

If Rice did have a daily to type, he probably wouldn't hit one correct key. His mind and heart would be with us. But I didn't want to risk confusing Johnny by introducing a new face now.

I stepped back into London's office, my composure miraculously restored. The sympathetic, understanding Reilly leaned toward Floyd, who cupped his face in his hands and sobbed pathetically. I sat behind the desk and watched.

"Has this asshole finally decided to tell the truth, Reilly?"

"He says he's really been in bad shape the last few months, but he's been trying to work out his problems. He says he probably bragged about the murders, but only because he was loaded. He says he didn't know Robinson, but he might have seen Hines in the Quarter. Do we have a picture of Hines? One we can show him?''

"Sure. Let me see what we have."

I walked outside to the big cabinets housing case files stored in thick brown folders, intending to pull an eight-by-ten portrait of Hines I'd removed from the Governor Nicholls apartment. Before my rummaging uncovered that photo, I noticed the small manila envelope containing the crime-scene pictures.

A malicious thought, a lightning stroke, came to me: *If Floyd wants to see Bill Hines, let him see the way he left him.*

I selected two of the grisliest shots: one depicting multiple stab wounds, the smeared, dried blood everywhere on the victim's body; the other a close-up of the neck wound with Hines almost decapitated. Photos a jury would never see because they were too hideous.

I thought about the way Floyd referred to victims by locations, how he talked about individuals not deserving to live, and his opinion of people not really being people.

It might work. What I had in mind might crack him.

I returned to the room and stepped around Reilly. Floyd's hands had become fists in front of his eyes, and his head slumped. I held the photo six inches below the fists, right underneath the lowered eyes. "Here, Floyd," I said. "Here's a picture of Bill Hines. Take a look at it. See if you recognize this man."

He looked, then quickly turned away. His face threatened to crumble into a thousand pieces.

I held the second photo down, the close-up of the neck. "Look at this one, Mr. Crazy Johnny. Take a good look."

Instead he glanced up, grabbed the picture from my hands, and held it in front of his eyes. He stared transfixed for a few moments. Then he turned to me, smiled sweetly, and said in the most reasonable voice, "Yeah, I did it. What do you want to know?"

"Just a minute," I said. Geesus, I hated this part. In a minute he might not be willing to talk. But I had to interrupt to arrest him, read him *Miranda* again, and have him sign an NOPD rights-of-arrestee form waiving his right to have an attorney present.

Currently unemployed, John Floyd had lived in the French Quarter off and on for ten years. He occasionally worked as a furniture repairman, a roustabout, and a clerk in a supermarket. Married as a teenager, he separated from his wife early on and drifted to New Orleans, with occasional forays taking him as far away as California. The *Times-Picayune* would call him a drifter, a transient, and the newspaper had it right. He spent the past year strung out on whiskey, which he drank on top of PCP.

Floyd said he met Bill Hines on Bourbon Street—he believed it was late on the Monday night prior to Thanksgiving—while "Hines stood near a lamppost." He told Hines he had no money and was looking for someone to buy him a drink. I could imagine the smiling, soft-spoken drifter snowing the lonely, gentle, older man.

They drank until 3 A.M., hitting several bars, and then Johnny asked if he could crash at Hines's apartment. He hid his true persona behind a hard-luck tale of losing his job and waiting for rescue money from home.

"He felt sorry for me," Johnny said.

Floyd remembered Hines having to unlock a large iron gate to enter a courtyard, and gave a detailed layout of the apartment where early that Tuesday morning they had a nightcap. He even told us what they drank—Jack Daniel's—from the glasses left on the kitchen table.

JOHN DILLMANN

I hounded Floyd for every scrap of information. When the confession got challenged—confessions are always challenged—I wanted proof he'd been in that apartment. With Reilly listening, I squeezed out every detail.

After several drinks, Johnny said, the scene turned ugly. It happened "in a flash," giving Hines no time to react. Johnny got into an argument with his benefactor, took a knife out of his boot, and plunged it into the victim's chest. He remembered Hines screaming. I hoped he'd never forget.

"I just flipped out," Floyd said, and recalled stabbing his victim "a few times." On this point he either lied or forgot, and I leaned to the latter. A mind might blot out the horror of what had happened, especially the bloody near-decapitation. In fact, further questioning suggested that Floyd blacked out during each murder, and afterward also.

Time and again Crazy Johnny said he confessed "because I'm sick and not responsible for my actions. I'm very ill and need help. When I mix drugs and booze I go mad." I didn't try to dissuade him from the truly insane belief that this was the perfect justification for murder.

But what hurt his future chances in court most was his ability to recall details of the apartment. He grew impatient when I asked him the location of bookshelves, the refrigerator, the kitchen table, believing I wasted his time with trivia. Floyd even described accurately what Hines wore that night.

"Did you steal anything?" I asked.

He wanted to hear this kind of question. "No," he said proudly. "I'm not a thief."

"What did you do after you killed Bill Hines?"

"I ran. I closed the door behind me and ran."

"Where did you go?"

"To a bar."

"Which bar?"

"I don't remember. I went to a bar and drank."

"You went straight from a killing binge to a drinking binge?"

"Yes."

No. Surely, no. Not even the Quarter's worst dive would ignore a customer soaked in blood. I let Floyd's answer go unchallenged. The truth would come soon enough.

"What kind of knife did you use?"

"A Buck knife. It has a six-inch blade and a wooden handle."

"What did you do with it?"

"I think I left it at Governor Nicholls. Or maybe I threw it away while I ran."

Tears glistened in Floyd's eyes through all of this. Remorse didn't show; the killer who's sorry is extremely rare. And he's only sorry because he got caught. Crazy Johnny's tears, if genuine, shone because he envisioned a tough time ahead for himself, treatment for alcoholism, drug addiction, and mental problems. "I guess I'll have to," he said, talking about the various programs, "but I'm not looking forward to it."

"How many people did you tell about killing Hines?"

"Dozens. Anybody who'd listen. Anybody I sat next to in a bar. But most of them thought it was just drunk talk."

"Did you stab the tourist in the Fairmont?"

"Yeah. But after that I sobered up, and went to the Detox Center. I'm harmless now."

"Did you continue taking drugs?"

"I got this mental problem."

Reilly and I stepped outside the office, told an elated Rice that he could have Johnny for the Robinson confession, and received hearty handshakes from a beaming Steve London, who came in upon hearing the heater might be broken. Then I called Diane.

"The case is cleared."

"I'll bet you're tired."

"I'm exhausted."

"Was it the person you thought?"

"Yes."

"Maybe we can take a few days together."

"I promise, Diane."

"You coming home now?"

"No. Rice is with him. I'll stay to see how that goes."

I also needed to type up Floyd's statement and have him sign it, a pleasant job. The miserable part, what I truly despised, was ordering dinner for him (in this case, chicken), watching him eat it, and listening to his small talk. I'd have to spend my own money to feed him—the department wouldn't spring for the meal, and a defense attorney would love to say I starved Johnny, thus tainting the confession—and be forced to choke back everything I felt about the motherfucker.

Back in London's office, Rice was just warming up. Even the streetwise Mike seemed disconcerted, not accustomed to a man who smiled while the foulest bile poured from his mouth, but obviously he'd begun to adapt. Rarely did Rice glimpse Johnny number three, the one who cried.

I sat in the chair Reilly previously occupied and listened. London's office seemed quiet compared to the buzzing homicide room I'd just left, alive with the news that we'd broken the big case.

Several days after the Hines murder, Crazy Johnny said, he met a black male walking on Orleans Street toward Bourbon, very early in the morning. This meant Robinson had changed his mind about having a nightcap.

"What happened?" Rice said. He had slipped into his what-the-hell-this-is-nothing role, acting like butchering someone in the Fairmont Hotel ranked right between jaywalking and spitting on the sidewalk.

"I stopped the dude," Floyd said, "and asked if he'd buy me a drink. We talked awhile, then he said, 'Sure,' and we went to The Pub. He bought me a whiskey. We talked some more and I told him I had no place to stay. He seemed real sorry for me. He said I could stay with him."

They walked to Robinson's car (Floyd didn't remember where it was parked, nor his victim's name), and drove to "near the Fairmont."

This was critical. "Where did Robinson park his car?"

"I don't remember exactly. Near the Fairmont."

"In the parking lot?"

"No. On the street."

Another important detail. He'd been there.

"How did you get into the Fairmont?"

"Through the front entrance. We walked up the steps and into the lobby."

"Were there any people in the lobby?"

"Several. We didn't pay any attention to them."

"What happened next?"

"We took the elevator and went real high up, it seemed, and walked a long way in the corridor. I followed the black dude into his room."

"What happened then?"

"I'm having trouble remembering. I was so messed up. I'd swallowed LSD an hour before—I must have blanked out. Then I was stabbing him. I just went berserk."

"How many times did you stab him?"

"Two or three."

"What did you do then?"

"I ran to the elevator and took it down. I ran through the lobby and out the door. I got to Bourbon Street, saw a guy I didn't know, told him I'd just killed a dude, and asked him to take me to Detox."

Amazing. After butchering Rodney Robinson, Floyd suffered a twenty-five-hour blackout, the actual length of time before he ran into Gerald Griffin and asked for assistance in getting to Charity Hospital.

"Did the guy go with you to Detox?"

"Yeah. He stayed awhile and then left."

"What kind of knife did you use?"

"All I know, it was about seven inches long, with a wood handle."

"Was it the knife you used on Hines?"

"I don't know. I don't think so. I had some other knives that week."

"What did you do with the knife?"

"I left it in the hotel room. Or maybe I threw it away while I ran toward Bourbon Street."

Rice questioned Floyd closely about details of the Fairmont Hotel room. Only someone who'd been there would remember where the drinks were left on the nightstand and the color of the room's carpet.

After Floyd answered all our questions, Mike and I typed up his respective statements, had him read them carefully and sign each page. While this went on the news media and various police brass got wind of the breakthrough. Phones rang incessantly.

I knew when we finished and strolled the Hollywood Walk— the section of White Street between Homicide and Central Lockup—with our prisoner, that TV would record our journey. I didn't know, couldn't have known, that a Channel 8 camera would play an absolutely critical role at the trial.

≡ **14** ≡

Violence had a good run in 1981. The feel-good era of the Reagan administration began with the release of our fifty-two hostages, held in Teheran for 444 days, but was shattered two months later when John Hinckley shot the President, Jim Brady, and two police officers at the side entrance of the Washington Hilton Hotel in Washington, D.C. Then, on May 13, Pope John Paul II was shot as he drove through the crowds in St. Peter's Square. In July there was a picturesque pause as most of the Western world tuned in to watch Prince Charles take the lovely Lady Diana as his bride in the first televised-live royal wedding. That October, Egyptian President Anwar Sadat was assassinated in Cairo during a military parade.

Back home, the Dodgers beat the Yankees four games to two in the World Series, "Physical" by Olivia Newton-John had just hit the charts, and Crazy Johnny sat in his cell in Central Lockup, awaiting trial for murder.

John Floyd's trial opened January 5, 1982, almost a year after his confessions, in Criminal District Court, Parish of Orleans, Judge Jerome M. Winsberg presiding.

It figured to be the kind of trial I like to attend, though

this one would hold no joy for me, because *all* the facts promised to come out in full-blooded debate. Both prosecution and defense agreed that a judge, without a jury, would hear the evidence. John Floyd's fate rested wholly in Judge Winsberg's hands.

I've never left a jury trial entirely satisfied. The jury doesn't hear a lot of the evidence, and much of the drama unfolds with them out of the courtroom. Facts get obfuscated as one side or the other grandstands, resorts to histrionics, relies on tricks—anything to sway the jury. The first casualty is usually truth as motions, objections, and technical rulings dilute what people need to know and understand to render a fair verdict.

Trials often become theater, entertaining to watch but not necessarily conducive to determining the truth. I've always thought these murder cases, with lives already lost and another life on the line, packed sufficient drama for anyone. The facts inevitably proved more interesting than the fiction each side felt compelled to suggest.

Judge Winsberg had the reputation of being an eminently fair jurist, and there was no reason why his ears, unlike a jury's, couldn't hear exactly what had happened. The bearded Winsberg looked younger than his forty years; owned a quick, probing mind; and long ago had built the reputation of doing what the law and his intellect told him was right. He would toss a case out in the wink of an eye if he thought the prosecution was off base and always acted in a pleasant, respectful manner, regardless of his inner feelings.

Courtroom regulars remember a pornography case Judge Winsberg heard: the prosecution of a New Orleans theater owner for showing a dirty movie. Winsberg, sitting on the bench reading a copy of the *Times-Picayune*, counted ads by fifteen other cinemas running the same film.

"Why aren't these others in court also?" he asked the

prosecutor. When no answer was offered, the proceedings became part of history's ash heap with a "case dismissed."

Indeed, Floyd's became a trial for purists, minus any showboating, needless motions, nitpicking objections, and snide asides.

Such a situation suited defense attorney Walter Sentenn just fine. *He'd* asked for the judge, believing deeply in his client's innocence, and feared rolling the dice with a jury. A jury, unpredictable, not always coldly logical, might be unduly impressed by a stream of police officers testifying for the prosecution, and by the bestial nature of the crimes.

Not a judge. Especially not Judge Winsberg, with his reputation for ruling strictly on the evidence. And Sentenn came armed to the teeth with powerful evidence—complicated material, needing explanation in scientific jargon, perhaps difficult for the average summoned citizen to understand—that convinced him the wrong man sat in the dock.

A big man, six foot three and powerfully built, thirty-seven years old, Sentenn spoke with a deep, powerful Roman senator's voice that impressed in casual conversation and overwhelmed in the courtroom. People *believed* Walter Sentenn when he employed his marvelous authoritative delivery.

Sentenn weighed in as a formidable opponent. A blue-collar lawyer, direct as a punch in the face, he attended law school at night for four years to obtain his degree, then joined the District Attorney's office upon graduation. He knew exactly what to expect from the prosecution.

Sentenn had a sense of humor—he played Santa Claus at the District Attorney's Christmas Party—and the self-assurance needed to poke fun at himself. He enjoyed recalling his early years in the prosecutor's office, when he handled so many cases, often simultaneously, that once he walked into a courtroom and began delivering his closing argument to an increasingly puzzled-looking jury. He'd orated in the wrong courtroom, to the wrong jury, about the wrong case.

Married to a former high school math teacher turned lawyer, Sentenn built an outstanding record as a prosecutor—former associates had difficulty recalling any case he had lost—before establishing an impressive reputation operating for the other side.

According to Louisiana law, when the crime in question is a capital offense and the defendant can't afford representation, the presiding judge can appoint any attorney he thinks will give the best defense. He even has the right to pull one out of private practice. As a result Sentenn, a top-notch criminal lawyer, was defending Johnny Floyd *pro bono*—for free.

The evidence—all credit to him for obtaining it—told this forceful man that John Floyd's case was a winner. Only one thing bothered him. Floyd had what Sentenn called "the Jimmy Carter Syndrome": he'd relate something outrageous, shocking, and horrifying through an incongruously innocent, angelic smile.

Judge Winsberg, reasoned Sentenn, had observed Floyd in pretrial hearings and could overlook his strange behavior, while a jury might automatically link Floyd to the stereotypical mass murderers they saw in cheap horror movies.

Sentenn thought long and hard before requesting a judge trial. He had the rare trait of being able to measure his own strengths and decided to forfeit two trump cards for the sake of a winning hand. One was the courtroom trick he'd mastered of "trying a case twice." During voir dire (the questioning of prospective jurors), if his slipped-in questions pertaining to the upcoming case elicited negative responses, he'd dismiss the juror. Giving up this weapon all lawyers employ but few use so well and his ability to sway a jury with his beautiful barrister's baritone, attested to Sentenn's confidence in his client's cause.

Assistant District Attorney David Plavnicky was equally content with Judge Winsberg. He held the one big card, maybe the ace of trumps: those confessions. Confessions are hard to beat. They set forth the defendant's own words implicating himself, admissions against interest—the best indicator of truth, but rightly not considered conclusive.

Unfortunately, defense attorneys usually try to discredit confessions by saying they have been beaten out of their clients. In past cases I had been accused of almost every conceivable barbarous act, including placing a plastic bag over a suspect's head, dangling a suspect out a window (the window in London's office that didn't open), punching suspects, torturing them, banging their heads against a wall—everything.

A lot of smoke in these instances didn't mean fire, and I doubt if the homicide detective exists who hasn't been accused of Torquemada-like brutality. It's the best way to get a confession thrown out. But hearing the charges hurled at me in case after case, week after week, year after year, depressed and angered me.

I often wondered what my children, or anyone, for that matter, would think if they read the transcripts of the hundreds of murder trials in which I participated, thousands of pages constituting an uninterrupted account of savage depravity. If just one of those allegations were true, I had no business working in any police department; in fact, I should be locked up.

"It's part of the job," said every one of my homicide commanders, and I suppose it is. But listening to unimaginably vicious killers trying to save their own skins by relating my inhumanity, and hearing pillar-of-the-community defense lawyers parrot the accusations as gospel truth in public hearings—to juries, to reporters—never went down easy.

I knew many jurors seriously wondered about the accusations, and I counted myself lucky that Judge Winsberg was hearing this case. He knew my reputation and work. I suspected that in this case—with its lack of physical evidence and extraordinary reliance on confessions—I'd be subjected to an all-out attack for the way I dealt with Floyd in London's office.

Plavnicky stood in my corner, but not to guard my interests, only to see his case not blow up. John Floyd didn't sue me for civil damages, in which instance I'd be a principal in the trial, with my own lawyer protecting my interests. Plavnicky had larger concerns than my feelings, and probably felt I should have learned how to take it by now. Besides, he bore his own cross. A district attorney finds himself steadily bombarded with all manner of accusations about unethical, immoral, and illegal practices, such as withholding or manufacturing evidence and encouraging witnesses to lie.

On the surface Plavnicky seemed overmatched by Sentenn. Tall and youthful, just three years out of law school (Tulane, considered the best in the South), he'd been thrown into a major homicide trial that promised to be loaded with land mines. Most D.A.'s, to protect a won/lost record upon which much of their ability is judged, prefer walkovers, open-and-shut cases almost impossible to bungle.

Mike Rice and I thought Plavnicky would do just fine. We'd seen some of the best prosecutors excel at an early age; they honed a natural cutting edge in the D.A.'s office—never lacking for a heavy caseload—and then went on to successful and more lucrative private practices.

Plavnicky, a handsome six-footer weighing two hundred pounds, walked with purposeful strides and seemed equally comfortable when serious or joking. He didn't put on the airs of some newcomers and socialized with a group of young assistant D.A.'s he considered "regular guys," not the yuppies, the climbers, the ones who thought book learning enough and experience irrelevant. Plavnicky occasionally hoisted a beer in Miracle Mile, the police hangout, and was always open to suggestions. In fact, he sought advice.

So the players were in place this January 5, with the main actor's freedom at stake on two counts of second-degree murder. To sustain a first-degree murder charge in Louisiana, the accused must have (1) killed during the commission of a felony (we suspected but couldn't prove John Floyd robbed his victims); (2) committed multiple simultaneous homicides; or (3) slain a law enforcement officer.

Premeditation doesn't count in distinguishing between first- and second-degree murder. However, sentencing varies only in that the defendant cannot receive the death penalty for second-degree murder. If found guilty, Floyd faced life imprisonment, with no chance of parole for forty years.

Friends of William Hines, relatives of Rodney Robinson, the press, murder-trial junkies, and other lawyers—both defense and prosecution, lured by the rare promise of a case up for grabs—crowded into the courtroom. The homicide addicts, particularly, possessed a sixth sense for divining the sites of dramatic trials. They consisted of old and young alike, men and women, some with night jobs, who seemed to ask, Why watch Perry Mason when we can see the real thing?

The lawyers from both ends of the spectrum were drawn by word of mouth that the shrewd Sentenn had something up his sleeve, that this highly publicized case (by inference "solved" with John Floyd's arrest) might end up with police and prosecution wearing egg on their faces.

Judge Winsberg set a brisk pace. He began by asking John Floyd if he indeed wanted trial by judge, and was answered in the affirmative. The blond Floyd, clean-cut in jacket and tie, could have stepped straight off the set of a soap opera where he played the good guy—a defense advantage lost when Sentenn made the hard but necessary choice of Judge Winsberg.

The first witness couldn't show. Assistant Coroner Monroe Samuels had been called out of town on business, and the results of his autopsies were stipulated into evidence by both sides, thus saving a good deal of time. In a jury trial Plavnicky would have pried every horrible detail of the butcherings out of Samuels, with Sentenn firing back a blizzard of objections. Winsberg didn't need this; he could read Dr. Samuels's reports.

Bill Hines's friend Thomas Bloodworth, the first prosecution witness, testified briefly and to the point. He related the circumstances leading to the discovery of Hines's body and, more importantly, identified the victim for the record. More than a year after learning of his coworker's murder, Bloodworth was still shaken when he talked about that terrible day. I guessed he would remember it always, as I would.

Carol Rodriguez, Robinson's seventh-grade teacher, performing a necessary formality, identified Rodney from a picture. In a jury trial, Plavnicky might have called a relative to make the identification, perhaps the grandmother, Kete Camel, knowing that the chances were excellent that someone close to Rodney would break down in tears. That would impress a jury. It would only irritate Judge Winsberg.

The prosecution didn't come armed with a great deal of evidence other than those confessions, but it did have some. Gerald G. Griffin, the offshore roustabout who'd first put me on to John Floyd, testified about his early morning encounter with the defendant on November 29, 1980: "Well, we chatted for a couple of minutes. I didn't pay much attention to how long. He stated that he had been messed up for several days, and wanted to go to the Detox Center at Charity Hospital. He asked me if I would go with him. At one point he mentioned he'd been treated in some type of mental facility a couple of times. He said he heard that checking into the Detox Center would be the next best thing, to keep from being held accountable for doing something wrong."

"Did you have a further conversation?" Plavnicky asked.

"He wondered if I'd heard about the stabbing at the Fairmont."

Next, Plavnicky called Steven Edwards, the forty-one-year-old owner of the Mississippi River Bottom bar. Relating exactly what he had told Reilly and me, Edwards testified that on November 29, 1980, the same day Griffin walked John Floyd to the Detox Center, he saw Floyd at 2 P.M.: "He was walking toward the bar and I said, 'Johnny, you know you're barred from the fucking bar.' I said, 'You can't go in there; I don't want you in there because you cause problems.' And he said, 'Don't come fucking with me. I already wasted one person.' I had just got through reading about Bill Hines, and I said, 'Who? Bill Hines?' and he said, 'Yeah, on Governor Nicholls.' I said, 'I don't give a shit. Get away from here.' He turned and left."

"Why was he known as 'Crazy Johnny'?" asked Plavnicky.

"The only thing I'd speak of is, in my bar, when he got drinking heavily, he was wacko in a way. He caused a lot of problems."

A question to Griffin about the Robinson murder. An admission to Edwards that he killed Hines. Next came an admission that he also killed Robinson.

Gene Reed, the bindery worker with O'Donnell Brothers Printing and Office Supply, testified about his post-Christmas meeting with John Floyd: "He saw me one evening on my way home and wanted some money. He was feeling very good. When I refused to give him any, he said he'd take care of me like he did the one at the Fairmont."

I took the stand. I related the investigative steps that led to picking up John Floyd and obtaining his subsequent confession. Sentenn asked only a few questions about the savage beating I allegedly administered to his client. He knew he wouldn't get anywhere with me on this subject; besides, in what promised to be the highlight of the trial, he intended to put his client on the stand to relate the lurid details.

Mike Rice followed me in the witness box. Two murder cases, after all, were being tried here, and Rice told about his investigation into Rodney Robinson's murder. Sentenn, cross-examining, elicited from Rice that the skullcap found in the hallway contained the hairs of a black male.

The prosecution rested. Had this been the end of the trial, authorities at Angola State Prison would already be preparing Floyd's cell. I'd seen defendants convicted partially on the basis of jailhouse confessions to convicted felons, scum-of-the-earth types who hoped for favors in exchange for snitching on a cellmate. In Griffin, Edwards, and Reed we had law-abiding witnesses who sought nothing. Steven Edwards, in particular, testified most reluctantly, fearing reprisals from Johnny if he got acquitted.

Judge Winsberg ordered a recess for lunch, allowing the defense two hours to fine-tune its case. Plavnicky could have called other witnesses to testify how John Floyd talked about "drilling holes" in people's heads, but he deemed this overkill and not likely to impress the straight-ahead Winsberg.

Witnesses we wanted but never found would have put Rodney Robinson and John Floyd together in The Pub, or Floyd with Bill Hines at one of the bars they visited. I went to numerous drinking spots trying to establish the connection, but failed. I looked almost two months after the fact (we didn't arrest Floyd until January 19) and would have been surprised if I had been able to put the killer with the victim. Johnny wouldn't have called attention to himself with his crazy show then. Had he done so, he'd have received no invitations to spend the night—in fact, there would be no trial right now.

I watched Sentenn leave the courtroom. His confident demeanor gave me the impression he would happily pass on lunch to proceed with chewing up our case and spitting it out as the garbage he believed it was.

≡ **15** ≡

On the surface, this trial seemed tranquil, a gentlemen's agreement of civility and co-operation, as if the two sides were discussing a mutually beneficial change of rules at the country club.

In reality, no one wanted to alienate Judge Winsberg, and both sides knew the decision maker on Floyd's innocence or guilt would only become aggravated by the tricks and ploys every lawyer uses in his jury-bewitching legerdemain.

Thus, in this atmosphere of judicial decorum, prosecution and defense readily agreed to the expertise of Sentenn's first witness, Dr. Marvin Miller, a clinical psychiatrist. That Dr. Miller ranked as a leading authority in his field probably wouldn't have mattered if a jury were hearing the case. Someone, most likely the prosecution, would have fired off numerous questions.

The courtroom was abnormally quiet as spectators strained to hear a noted psychiatrist's assessment of the strange defendant in the dock.

SENTENN: Dr. Miller, were you appointed by this court to examine Mr. John Floyd for lunacy purposes, as to his present competency and his competency at the time of the commission of the crime?

MILLER: I was.

SENTENN: When did you make a report to this court?

MILLER: I rendered a written report to the court April 2, 1981.

SENTENN: And the substance of your opinion in that report?

MILLER: That Mr. Floyd, at the time I saw him, was competent to assist in his own defense and appreciate the nature of the charges against him, but that I was unable to make a statement or opinion about his mental status at the time of the alleged offenses for which he had been charged.

SENTENN: Why were you unable to offer such an opinion?

MILLER: Mr. Floyd advised that for an extended period—before, during, and after the times of the alleged offenses—he used, to paraphrase him, "every kind of street drug and drank regularly in bars in the French Quarter." As a consequence, he said he did not remember specifically where he had been on any particular day. He was, however, of the opinion that he had not committed the offenses for which he had been charged, and he advised as well that the confession which he apparently signed had, in fact, been signed under duress following his alleged beating by the police.

SENTENN: Was he able to indicate to you his mental

state at the time the confession was allegedly taken from him?

MILLER: No. He listed a variety of drugs by name that he had taken, some of which may have had lasting effects, may have caused flashbacks, and so on. So, I really had no way of trying, no way of checking or cross-checking his story to make a determination about his mental status; nor did he, because of the history he gave me, because of the denial of this alleged offense, and because of his statement of vagueness about that whole October, November, December period in his life.

SENTENN: Given Mr. Floyd's statement that he had been coerced into making the confessions, and given what you know of his background and his clinical time, are you able to offer any sort of considered opinion whether he could have been led into making those confessions, and whether he is susceptible to being led?

MILLER: Well, I'd say this at the outset: Depending on the nature of the alleged coercive force, anybody might sign a confession. I'd say, however, that based on his own statement, he was basically, to paraphrase him again, unclear about what he was doing and he felt scared. I'm referring to the period during which he was allegedly beaten, prior to his signing the confession. If, in fact, he were intoxicated, even subclinically, this well could have made him vulnerable to even minimal coercion. I would also say, given the life-style he described, given the fact that he was pretty much dependent on other people, and pretty much accountable to them as a consequence, that too would, in my opinion, provide him with a degree of vulnerability to suggestions, coercions, very likely greater than the average person not living in this particular life-style or abusing drugs and/or alcohol.

SENTENN: Did you get the impression from talking with him, and the information provided to you, that he was a street person, and had been living on the street and off of other people?

MILLER: Yes, he pretty much advised that after he and his wife split and he came to New Orleans, he worked intermittently, but he was pretty much a street person in the sense of having only transient relationships, drinking a lot, drinking with people who might have provided him alcoholic beverages, using drugs with people who might have provided him drugs. He was making his living, if you will, by accommodating to the wishes of other people, and in that sense, he was certainly a street person.

SENTENN: Did you detect any proclivity to violence on your person in your examination?

MILLER: Certainly not in the examination I conducted. I'm not quite sure what you mean, but he wasn't threatening in any way.

Dr. Marvin Miller certainly didn't testify as most psychiatrists do at murder trials. Often, each side presents a psychiatrist and the jury can take its pick: The man or woman for the prosecution expresses no doubt that the defendant is a vicious, cunning, cold-blooded murderer, certain to kill again, if released; the defense shrink talks about a troubled childhood and negative societal influences, but *knows* the accused to be constitutionally incapable of committing the crime charged.

Both psychiatrists are called whores by cynical insiders, including the police, because they sell their services to whomever bids for them. I can't recall a psychiatrist paid by the defense ever saying the defendant "is just a hard-down nasty son of a bitch." Nor has a prosecutor produced a psychiatrist who says, "This poor fellow is just crazy. He needs help. It would be barbaric to punish him."

Given the psychiatric polar opposites juries hear testifying, I didn't think these experts shed much light on the issues. In this instance, though, the judge originally had appointed Miller for the April 1981 lunacy hearing (Johnny had tried to beat the rap by pleading insanity, certainly within his rights, but *now* he claimed flat-out innocence), and I genuinely hoped for enlightenment from a highly respected professional beholden to neither side.

In addition, I had seen so few cases in which the psychiatrist came forward without bias that I wondered what this "objective scientist" would say. What truth would I hear from Dr. Miller?

Plavnicky rose to cross-examine:

PLAVNICKY: Dr. Miller, it's your testimony that you detected no proclivity toward violence on his part?

MILLER: I'm saying during the period I examined him, he was in no way threatening to me, nor did he demonstrate any emotional lability or any volatility period.

PLAVNICKY: Would you read this sentence from State's Exhibit Nineteen?

MILLER: Yes. This is from my report. He spoke as well of, "talking about killing people—putting holes in their heads," to his acquaintances, because of having read about the offenses in question in the newspaper.

PLAVNICKY: Dr. Miller, do you think that talking about putting holes in people's heads and killing people is indicative of possible proclivity toward violence?

MILLER: It's certainly a possibility.

PLAVNICKY: Now, Doctor, the fact he spoke to people about killing human beings, didn't that indicate to you he was a potentially violent person?

MILLER: No. My answer was about his behavior during the time he and I were together and I was interviewing him.

PLAVNICKY: Would that conversation indicate to you a man who has a possible capacity for violence?

MILLER: If I might answer this way: He said, "I go around talking about killing people when I drink and when I'm sober too sometimes." I would say, by his own words, by his own statement, he advised me he talked about killing people, but whether this was a function of intoxication, a losing of his consciousness with alcohol and/or drugs, or whether this is, in fact, a very specific proclivity or inclination of his, I don't know. I can only report on what he said. He did, in fact, say, "I go around talking about killing people when I drink and when I'm sober too, sometimes." But I would not want to draw inferences from that statement that this man is or isn't capable of violence.

PLAVNICKY: At the same time, you don't want this court to infer he is a man *not* capable of killing people?

MILLER: I think that's absolutely fair. I think what the court infers is up to the court. I don't feel comfortable from the psychiatric standpoint making inferences about somebody's violence potential based solely on that kind of statement. That's all I said.

So I learned what a psychiatrist owing allegiance to neither side would say. I had no quarrel with Dr. Miller. He did his best, probably as well as anyone on the planet could have done. But what purpose did this serve in a court of law? Who learned anything, became wiser, because of it?

PLAVNICKY: You also testified that during the course of your examination he admitted living off people in the French Quarter?

MILLER: Now, let me put it this way: That's an inference I drew, mainly that, not having a regular job, drinking and abusing drugs and so on, required his engaging in various kinds of activities that involved transient relationships with people.

PLAVNICKY: Did he tell you whether he maintained a regular address?

MILLER: I don't know that I asked him. I got the decided impression he lived in the Quarter with friends, and moved from one place to another.

PLAVNICKY: In your professional opinion, did he appear aware of the existence of his problems?

MILLER: Yes, I think he was fairly candid about it.

PLAVNICKY: Did he label his drug abuse as a problem?

MILLER: Yes. He said, for example, he'd been in a detox unit up at Charity Hospital in the recent past, and that certainly indicates someone's appreciation of the need for help.

PLAVNICKY: Now, Doctor, you weren't present at the time the defendant gave his confession, obviously?

MILLER: No.

PLAVNICKY: And you're not testifying whether his signature was obtained under duress, are you?

MILLER: No.

PLAVNICKY: It's certainly possible the defendant had this awful thing on his conscience and for therapeutic reasons confessed to the police voluntarily. Is that not possible?

SENTENN: I object, Your Honor. Outside of the purview of this doctor's expert opinion.

WINSBERG: If you can answer it in terms of your expertise, you may. Or you can beg off.

MILLER: No. I've stated and I hope clearly that—

PLAVNICKY: Well, Doctor, I'm going to ask if you could possibly answer my question with a yes or no, and then explain it.

MILLER: Yes, I think it's certainly possible somebody might be sufficiently aware of the magnitude of an event and, as a consequence of the guilt provoked by that event, confess voluntarily.

During redirect, Sentenn elicited that a person like John Floyd could more easily be coerced into a confession than, say, the average John Q. Citizen, not burdened with excess baggage and lack of self-respect.

I scored Dr. Miller's testimony a wash; maybe a slight advantage for the defense. Floyd certainly didn't present himself to the psychiatrist as the Crazy Johnny of our investigation. Also, Sentenn managed to portray Floyd as a person more likely than most to confess to a crime he didn't commit.

That might be true. But how did he know all those details of the crimes? That Jack Daniels had been the booze found at Hines's apartment? The color of the carpet in Robinson's hotel room?

Dr. Miller's testimony, as mentioned, differed from that heard at most murder trials: ambivalent, not doctrinaire. Maybe it hovered as close to the truth as we can know it, though I doubted that. I didn't believe Johnny confessed because he felt guilty. I sat with him, talked with him. I believed he confessed primarily (granted, the crime scene photo shook him to the soles of his feet) because he mistakenly thought we had the goods on him and reasoned he could beat the murder raps with an insanity plea.

Next Sentenn, still holding back his big guns, called Arthur Huddick, a clinical coordinator of the Alcoholism and Drug Abuse Program at Metairie General Hospital.

SENTENN: Do you know John Floyd?
HUDDICK: I've met John Floyd. I don't really know the man.

SENTENN: When did you meet him?

HUDDICK: I can't tell you the date. I can tell you how I met him. I was down at the St. Louis Community Center doing volunteer work, and he came in with DTs from some chemical. I decided he needed hospitalization. I took him in a taxicab to Charity Hospital, and they admitted him into their alcohol unit. They treated him, I guess, in the emergency room, and admitted him to their program. That was how we met.

SENTENN: Do you have any idea what month that might have occurred?

HUDDICK: Not really. It was over a year ago, and he wasn't a client, he was just someone who came in off the street, which is a constant thing there. We give out free sandwiches to a continuous flow of street people going through. That's why I don't remember the date.

SENTENN: Did you see him any time after that?

HUDDICK: Yes, I did. He called the Community Center. To the best of my recollection, he was being released from the hospital at Charity, after spending some time in their treatment program. I have a detox program and an alcohol program, and he said he was coming out and needed some support, social-service support, which the Community Center does have available, and he was aware it was available to him there. I told him there was a meeting Wednesday night, and that he should attend, if he was interested in staying clean and sober. I asked a few of my friends who went to that particular meeting whether any new people came that night. They said there wasn't anyone, that Floyd didn't show up.

After that episode, I was at a bar in the French Quarter, and John Floyd came inside. He appeared to be high on something, and I was really confrontive with him about being high on a drug. I don't talk to drug addicts that are using, and I told him to leave and get away from me. He got real belligerent, apparently out of control, yelling at me. I can't remember exactly what he said but I can give you the essence of my feelings. I was frightened, and I don't frighten easily. I felt threatened. It scared me. Later I saw John walking on the street a few times, and there was a definite Dr. Jekyll/Mr. Hyde kind of thing. He seemed very sick when I saw him the first time, but this was a totally different person.

SENTENN: Was he inebriated the second time?

HUDDICK: He was under the influence of something, alcohol or drugs. I felt it was drugs.

SENTENN: Do you know anything of his reputation in the French Quarter?

HUDDICK: I assumed John was a street person. I thought he was hustling. Other than that, a reputation? Not really. He was just among the many I see all the time.

SENTENN: Do you see a lot of street people in your job?

HUDDICK: Yes.

SENTENN: Do you see a lot of hustlers in your job?

HUDDICK: Not working with them directly, but I live

right in the heart of all that, so I do see a lot of people, yeah.

SENTENN: In your expert opinion, when a person of this nature is confronted with stress, a coercive attitude, are they inclined to be compliant and give in to whatever somebody wants them to say or do?

HUDDICK: If you're talking about my encounter with John—

SENTENN: I'm asking, do street people of that nature, hustlers who are also alcoholics or drug abusers, when they are confronted with a stressful, coercive circumstance, either by an authority figure or something similar, are they inclined to give in and do whatever that authority figure wants them to do?

HUDDICK: It would really depend on the drugs they use. I've seen compliance, and I've seen belligerence, depending on the person, how that person reacts to the particular drug they're taking, the synergistic effect of the drugs on the biochemical make-up. A whole bunch of things apply. I can't give you a set answer. It would depend on the particular person, his use of a particular drug, how it affects him at that particular moment.

SENTENN: Would it be easier to cope with alcohol than with drugs?

HUDDICK: Again, no. It goes from one end of the spectrum to the other. I've seen alcoholics who become very compliant when confronted with an authority figure, and I've seen others act real belligerent, but the similarity is, their reality is very dilutive, so they're not, as far as I'm concerned, perceiving the same real-ity as the person that's confronting them.

SENTENN: So the person in that circumstance would not necessarily know what is going on about him, being confronted by an authority fig-ure?

HUDDICK: In a drugged state, if he's drugged.

SENTENN: How does that effect their ability to react and to respond?

HUDDICK: They're not getting or receiving informa-tion. Well, they're receiving information, but they're receiving it through a system that's drug-affected. So they give a drug-affected response to whatever the input is. And, depending again on what—if they're alcoholic, if they are drug addicts—they're using at that moment, or coming off a drug, or whatever.

SENTENN: Would you, in your expert opinion, classify John Floyd as an alcoholic?

HUDDICK: I don't know that much about John. In my encounters with him, he's been under the influence of drugs and alcohol.

SENTENN: Would you classify him as a substance abuser?

HUDDICK: I've seen John abuse substances. I would have to know John's history, and his rela-tionship to the drugs. I couldn't give you that answer, I'm sorry.

Plavnicky had a few points to make.

PLAVNICKY: You say it was your impression that Mr. Floyd was hustling?

HUDDICK: By hustling, I meant hustling money, asking people for money on the street. He asked me for money once on the street. I have to walk up Bourbon Street to get to my house, and I often get asked for money. I usually send them to the Center, if they're hungry, to get food.

PLAVNICKY: And you state that the time you saw him in the bar, he became very belligerent to you?

HUDDICK: Right off the bat. He lost it. He was just not rational.

PLAVNICKY: At that point he did appear capable of doing violence?

HUDDICK: Well, I felt threatened. I was scared and felt he could be violent at that moment.

PLAVNICKY: You were afraid of violence being directed at yourself?

HUDDICK: Yes. And it was not an extreme reaction. I'm not a person who scares easily, so if I reacted scared, I know at that moment I was scared.

I didn't see how Huddick advanced John Floyd's cause. He didn't know if the defendant was the type to confess readily to a crime he didn't commit, and his portrait of Floyd bordered on the chilling. Huddick appeared to be someone not easily intimidated, yet Floyd shook him to his foundations. I believed Huddick had glimpsed a small part of the terrifying beast who suddenly confronted and annihilated William Hines and Rodney Robinson.

But Sentenn had only warmed up his engines. Huddick said he didn't know; he didn't say that Floyd was a mentally tough, harder-than-granite block an atom smasher couldn't break.

Now, in a startling deviation from the norm, Sentenn called four witnesses who would ordinarily testify for the state: Alan Sison, NOPD criminalist; Daniel Waguespack, NOPD criminalist; Patricia Daniels, medical technician employed by the Orleans Parish Coroner's Office; and security guard Nedra Boykin.

Plavnicky knew these witnesses would be called and that their testimony might be devastating, but found himself powerless to counter. Sentenn, a brilliant master of ceremonies, whisked them center stage in the courtroom and adroitly, succinctly, and logically elicited what they had to say, what the man who counted—Judge Winsberg—would certainly find impressive. These four witnesses were why Sentenn had passed on a jury trial.

Nedra Boykin, of course, cast a dark cloud over the Fairmont murder with testimony about the black man running from the service elevator smack into her guard's cage, just about the time of the homicide.

Winsberg might write Boykin's testimony off as coincidence, but what about Sentenn's other three star witnesses, Sison, Waguespack, and Daniels?

They testified about the hairs of a black male found in that skullcap, not in itself devastating evidence. A Fairmont employee might have dropped it; it could have come from anywhere. Even Sentenn didn't dwell on it.

Then Sentenn dropped his bombshell: blood, *type A*, discovered in Fairmont Room 1029. *Floyd's blood type was B, Robinson's type, AB.*

Sentenn had gambled and won: Floyd told the lawyer he was innocent, and Sentenn believed him. After warning Johnny of the danger—"You're *sure* you want me to go ahead?"—Sentenn had Johnny's blood analyzed. He could have lost big, had it matched the samples taken from the hotel room. Instead, he hit the jackpot.

As policemen, our hands were bound. We couldn't force the defendant to give blood for testing, and Johnny's medical records were hard to trace, so we were in the dark. Somehow, we were certain the blood would match. We were wrong.

How could that type A blood found in Rodney Robinson's Fairmont room be explained? I asked myself over and over again. It must belong to someone else, an earlier guest, or a second killer. Or, Sentenn contended, logic on his side, the actual killer—obviously not John Floyd.

I didn't believe it for a minute. I had taken Floyd's confession and listened to him describe details of the Hines and Robinson murders only the killer could know: the apartment layout, the Jack Daniels, the two cocktail glasses on the table, the Fairmont room's carpet color, the fact Robinson parked on the street.

Could someone else have murdered Robinson? Could our perception of the cases and our single-murderer presumption have been flawed from the beginning?

Sending the wrong man to prison is every thinking detective's nightmare. The prosecutor, not the police, must prove the defendant guilty, but no officer with a whit of decency fails to thoroughly investigate any alternative.

Since learning about the type A blood, I agonized over the possibility of being wrong. I rehashed the case endlessly, nights with Diane and days over quick lunches or coffee with Fred or Mike Rice. I admit I had to fight the tendency to despise John Floyd. He was the ugliest kind of braggart, a belligerent drunk, an addict, and an unpredictable bully, beaming angelic virtue one moment and sprouting horns and fangs the next. I attempted to dissociate myself from this knowledge; to try and think it *didn't* matter. But the truth is that no matter how hard I tried, I still believed his talk about killing people amounted to more than blowing wind.

It always came down to John Floyd. I remembered the

intensity of his sobbing confession, related with absolute authority, how he snapped out answers about the clothes Hines wore as they barhopped, the Jack Daniels they drank, parking Robinson's car on the street. *We had kept these details and more from the press.* Only the killer could have answered our questions correctly.

What about that type A blood? I'll wonder about it always. A hundred circumstances, every one unlikely, could explain it. The one I finally arrived at shakily, after an elaborate process of elimination I never verbalized: the crime lab made a mistake. It had happened before in rare instances. They had inadvertently mixed up blood samples from another case with this one.

Darkness had fallen outside when Judge Winsberg recessed the trial for the day. Tomorrow morning the witness stand would feature the grand finale, John Floyd himself, trying to save his skin—if Walter Sentenn hadn't already.

There would be no closing arguments, no stirring speeches, no pulse-quickening rhetoric from Sentenn or Plavnicky. Dramatic oratory would be wasted on Winsberg. When Johnny finished, the judge would retire to his chambers, then likely return shortly to render his verdict.

≡ **16** ≡

Usually extraneous noises ruf-
fle a courtroom: spectators moving about, feet shuffling,
coughs, whispers. Judge Winsberg's court this morning of January 6, 1982, with John Floyd on the witness stand, was as
quiet as a monastery at midnight.

Diane, who rarely attended my case trials, came to hear
Crazy Johnny. I had talked so much about him, our strange
investigation, and the terrible murders, she decided to see for
herself.

I would have chosen almost any other trial for her to attend. The defense always portrayed me as moral slime, and I
knew Dillmann-according-to-Floyd would match or surpass
the all-time character assassinations. Type A blood or not,
this case was still up for grabs. Why else would Johnny take
the stand? Floyd had his entire life to save, and save it he
would if he could beat those confessions by slandering me.

Floyd in jacket and tie could pass as an aging preppie, till
he started talking and became rural Mississippi. Sentenn
gambled putting him on the stand; the lawyer figured he had
won the Robinson part of the case, of the Hines murder he
couldn't be sure. Still, he knew as well as I that the prose-

cution contended heart and soul that we dealt with two killings and one killer. If this got extended to its logical
conclusion—and Sentenn believed the evidence proved Floyd
couldn't have murdered Robinson—the defendant stood innocent of both crimes.

Johnny had an alibi for the Hines homicide. Rating alibis
on a scale of one to ten, it scored a one, and Sentenn knew
it. Still, Johnny stuck to his story. He *wanted* to testify. And
he had been right before: He had urged the reluctant lawyer
to type those blood samples.

So Sentenn let Johnny testify. It was, after all, Floyd's life
at stake. The lawyer warned of the dangers implicit in the
tale Johnny intended to weave, but the defendant insisted.

Floyd had half of a bus ticket sold in San Francisco on
November 20, 1980. He'd spent six weeks working odd jobs
in California. If he took the next bus, which he said he did,
and stayed on it (he said he didn't), he would have arrived
in New Orleans on November 23, in plenty of time to murder
Bill Hines in the early morning hours of November 25.

But Floyd swore he was still on the bus.

SENTENN: When you got to San Antonio on the
twenty-second, what did you do? Did you stay
on the bus?

FLOYD: No, I got off the bus and started drinking in
the bar and missed the bus.

SENTENN: You missed the bus in San Antonio?

FLOYD: I stayed to the next day and caught the other
one.

SENTENN: What time did you catch the bus the next
day, the twenty-third, from San Antonio?

FLOYD: It was late in the evening.

SENTENN: How late in the evening? After five o'clock,
before five o'clock?

FLOYD: It was after five, I'm pretty sure.

SENTENN: Was it after ten o'clock?

FLOYD: No, it wasn't that late. It was between eight and ten.

SENTENN: When you got on the bus on the twenty-third, where did you go?

FLOYD: Houston.

SENTENN: How long did it take you to get from San Antonio to Houston?

FLOYD: It's maybe six hours. I'm not sure.

SENTENN: Did you get to Houston on the same day, the twenty-third, or did you get there on the twenty-fourth?

FLOYD: It was some time in the early morning of the twenty-fourth.

SENTENN: When you arrived on the twenty-fourth, did you stay on the bus or come to New Orleans?

FLOYD: I stayed in Houston.

SENTENN: Where in Houston did you stay?

FLOYD: At the bus station.

SENTENN: How long did you stay?

FLOYD: I was out drinking at the bars in the west part of Houston. So, it was around the twenty-fifth when I arrived in New Orleans, around one P.M.

SENTENN: What time did you leave Houston?

FLOYD: It was after midnight on the twenty-fifth.

Johnny's uncorroborated alibi, if believed, eliminated him as Hines's killer. He hadn't even been in town. Sentenn tried to find someone, anyone, who remembered Floyd in San Antonio or Houston, but I knew the odds he faced. I hadn't been able to connect the defendant with Hines or Robinson in the bars Johnny said they visited in New Orleans the

mornings of their murders. The story Johnny dished up—
missing two buses to get drunk—might be swallowed, if only
because it fit the man. What followed I couldn't imagine
anyone believing.

SENTENN: Your testimony is that you left the bus station about two P.M. on the twenty-fifth.
Where did you go from there?

FLOYD: To the Louisiana Purchase.

SENTENN: What did you do?

FLOYD: I started drinking.

SENTENN: Was anybody there that you knew?

FLOYD: A bunch of people. Carl the bartender, for
one.

But Carl didn't get called to the stand. No one from that
"bunch of people," who might have testified that he thought
it extremely unlikely Johnny murdered someone ten hours
before, came forward as witnesses. I knew the reason wasn't
for lack of Sentenn's trying.

SENTENN: When did you leave the Louisiana Purchase?

FLOYD: Late that night. I went to another bar.

SENTENN: What bar?

FLOYD: The Galley House. I stayed until it closed.

SENTENN: Where did you go from there?

FLOYD: I went over to Morris's house, the guy that
I was living with in the French Quarter.

SENTENN: Who was that?

FLOYD: Morris.

SENTENN: Morris who?

FLOYD: I can't pronounce his last name.

SENTENN: Can you spell it?

FLOYD: No.

SENTENN: Where did Morris live?

FLOYD: Ten eighteen Rampart.

SENTENN: Have you tried to contact him since you've been in jail?

FLOYD: Yes, sir. He wrote me letters and stuff, but he's moved.

SENTENN: Where did he move?

FLOYD: To Houston—Dallas, Texas.

SENTENN: Have you written and asked him to come back and testify for you?

FLOYD: Yeah. A couple of times. But I never did get any more answers from him. He don't want to get involved.

Unbelievable, and Sentenn knew it. *Didn't want to get involved?* If Morris I-can't-pronounce-his-last-name existed, it was stop-the-trial time for Floyd until he could be produced. Morris could save him. He could say he knew nothing about knives and bloody discarded clothes, how Johnny, returning early the morning of November 26, told him about the bus ride adventure, and he could swear that Johnny had been away the nights of the twenty-third and twenty-fourth.

Didn't want to testify? Sentenn would move heaven and earth to find this character and lay a subpoena on him.

I thought the mention of the mysterious Morris counted as a defense disaster. His lawyer warned him it likely would come out that way (Sentenn had done everything possible to locate the witness), but Floyd insisted his way was best.

Crazy Johnny had an alibi for the Robinson killing, also. It was none other than Gene Reed, who Floyd said lied in court when he testified "he'd take care of me like he did the one at the Fairmont."

SENTENN: Was that your potential alibi, that you were with Gene on Thanksgiving night?

FLOYD: All that night and the next morning.

SENTENN: What kind of condition was Gene in?

FLOYD: He was drunk. He couldn't walk.

SENTENN: So you're saying he just can't remember?

FLOYD: He can't remember.

SENTENN: Where did you go when you woke up Friday?

FLOYD: To the Louisiana Purchase.

SENTENN: Were you meeting someone?

FLOYD: One of the bartenders: Carl.

SENTENN: Why were you meeting him?

FLOYD: He's a friend of mine. We drink together.

SENTENN: This friend Carl, what's his last name?

FLOYD: I can't recall it right now.

SENTENN: Do you know where he lives?

FLOYD: He lives on Barracks Street, on the corner of Barracks and Dauphine.

SENTENN: Does he still live there?

FLOYD: There ain't been nobody able to find either one of the bartenders.

SENTENN: Who was the other bartender?

FLOYD: His name was Bill. He was working the morning shift.

Next Floyd explained away Gerald Griffin.

SENTENN: Do you remember Gerald Griffin testifying yesterday? He said you mentioned the stabbing at the Fairmont.

FLOYD: Yes, sir.

SENTENN: Do you remember making that statement to him?

FLOYD: I read it in the paper, is what I did, over at Morris's house. I got a paper on Canal Street.

SENTENN: Did you tell him you committed the murder?

FLOYD: No, sir.

And no one said he did. Now Johnny turned to Steven Edwards.

SENTENN: This Steven Edwards, the one you talked to, about "wasting a guy around the corner." Do you remember that testimony?

FLOYD: Yes, sir. Well, not talking to him, because I never did. I remember him telling it yesterday.

SENTENN: You're saying you didn't tell him you wasted someone around the corner?

FLOYD: No, sir, because I'd never been back down there since I got barred. I saw him in the Docks and the Louisiana Purchase, but I never would talk to him.

The bell tolled for me. I was glad Diane heard what went before, because she was about to get an earful, an astonishing account of her husband's disregard for the law, his appalling arrogance, and his brutality.

SENTENN: At the time they handcuffed you and took you away, were you drunk?

FLOYD: Yes, sir, I was, because I had been drinking all that morning.

SENTENN: Had you taken any pills?

FLOYD: I took some Quaaludes before I left the apartment.

SENTENN: How many drinks had you taken when you were arrested?

FLOYD: I don't recall, but I had a good many, because I know John Reilly and them, they bought me about five or six beers.

SENTENN: Now, when you take Quaaludes and drink beers with it, does it have any effect on you?

FLOYD: Well, not really.

SENTENN: What kind of effect does it have on you?

FLOYD: It just makes me high. It doesn't make me drowsy or nothing like that.

SENTENN: It wouldn't make you drunk? Would you be able to talk, to walk?

FLOYD: Well, not really. I was staggering and stuff, because I took them that morning.

SENTENN: What time did you get to headquarters?

FLOYD: It was probably around two o'clock.

SENTENN: By the time you got out of the holding cell at five o'clock, were you sober?

FLOYD: Yes, sir.

SENTENN: By that time you had dried out pretty much?

FLOYD: Yes, sir. They kept me handcuffed the whole time I was in the holding cell.

SENTENN: Did you have a hangover?

FLOYD: Yes, sir. Real nervous feeling.

SENTENN: And what do you usually do about that?

FLOYD: Well, I either drink some more or take some more Quaaludes.

SENTENN: Do you recall when they began interrogating you?

FLOYD: It was after five o'clock.

SENTENN: Was that in an open office where people could come in and out?

FLOYD: No sir, closed in.

SENTENN: Were there windows people could see in?

FLOYD: There was a window overlooking the parking lot.

SENTENN: Any windows where the people in the office area itself could see in?

FLOYD: No, sir.

SENTENN: When you were interrogated, how many people were present?

FLOYD: Well, there was one lady, a colored lady, saw my face bleeding when the door was opened. She was sitting out in the front by a desk.

SENTENN: How many people actually interrogated you at any one time?

FLOYD: Well, there was mostly John Dillmann, John Reilly. Dillmann mostly threatened me and said some things.

SENTENN: Who first started talking to you? Did they both start?

FLOYD: Both of them started, and then John Reilly, he left.

SENTENN: What kind of questions did Dillmann ask you?

FLOYD: Well, he just told me, "I know you killed these people."

SENTENN: And what did you say?

FLOYD: I told him I didn't. He told me I was lying.

SENTENN: Did you kill those people?

FLOYD: No, sir.

SENTENN: Do you know those people?

FLOYD: No, sir.

SENTENN: What other questions did he ask you?

FLOYD: He just started asking me questions about did I do it, and I kept telling him I didn't, and that's when he started beating me.

— 237 —

SENTENN: How did he beat you?

FLOYD: He started slapping me on the side of the head, and hit me a bunch of times.

SENTENN: Slapped you on the side of the head with what?

FLOYD: His hand.

SENTENN: Open hand?

FLOYD: Yes, sir.

SENTENN: How many times did he slap you?

FLOYD: A couple of times, I guess. Maybe two or three, I'm not sure. It might have been more because he pulled some of my hair out.

SENTENN: Were you trying to attack him or to escape at the time?

FLOYD: No, sir.

SENTENN: Did he threaten you besides that?

FLOYD: Yes, sir.

SENTENN: In what way?

FLOYD: He threatened to put my head through the brick wall, and throw me out through the window to the parking lot. He said he could kill me and get by with it.

Diane's face had tensed; color drained from her lips. For a moment I got angry with *her*. Why did she insist on coming? I knew it would become worse, much worse, I had heard it all a hundred times; despair crept into the pit of my stomach.

Diane, eyes aglint—I'd never seen such a look—stared at the smiling man on the witness stand. *Geesus, Honey, he's lying,* I wanted desperately to say.

SENTENN: What was your reaction at the time?

FLOYD: Well, I was scared.

SENTENN: Did you believe him?

FLOYD: Yes, sir.

SENTENN: Why?

FLOYD: He meant business.

SENTENN: Did he do anything physical besides slapping you?

FLOYD: Yes, sir. He kicked me on the side of the head with his boots.

SENTENN: How did he manage to do that?

FLOYD: He was sitting in front of me in the chair. He hauled off. When I told him I didn't do it, he kicked me and knocked me off on the floor.

SENTENN: While you were sitting in the chair, you're saying that he kicked you in the head?

FLOYD: Yes.

SENTENN: When you were sitting upright in the chair?

FLOYD: Yes, sir.

SENTENN: How many times did he do that?

FLOYD: He only kicked me once, and then I think he hit me again while I was on the floor. I was so scared.

He was scared? I consoled myself that he should know about scared. I thought of William Hines and Rodney Robinson and the sweet-faced murderous liar on the witness stand.

SENTENN: Now, after he did that, did you make a statement?

FLOYD: Well, they asked me questions and stuff.

SENTENN: And how did he ask you questions?

FLOYD: He just started, you know, asking me where did I meet the guys at, did I meet them on

Bourbon Street, and I said, "Yes, I met them on Bourbon Street." I was repeating after them. I never did give any testimony.

SENTENN: What do you mean?

FLOYD: He would say something and I'd say, "Yes, that's the way it happened."

SENTENN: Did you ever offer any details to him?

FLOYD: No, sir. Well, I said I met the guy on Bourbon Street and walked over to the hotel. He said, "Did you walk him up to the room?" I said, "Yes."

SENTENN: Why did you do that? Why did you tell him these things?

FLOYD: Either do that or probably get killed or messed up, and I was scared.

SENTENN: Is what you were telling him the truth?

FLOYD: No, sir.

SENTENN: Did you tell him the truth? Did you ever try to tell him the truth?

FLOYD: Yes, sir. But he wouldn't listen to me. He was mad. Well, he acted like he had been drinking. He was upset about something.

SENTENN: John, you understand what you're doing now? You're saying you did not give that story or statement?

FLOYD: I might have given some of it, but not all of it.

SENTENN: What some of it did you give?

FLOYD: Well, I told him about me meeting a guy on Bourbon Street, and then he added to it, and I said, "That's what happened."

SENTENN: Was it true that you met a guy on Bourbon Street?

FLOYD: No, sir.

SENTENN:	Why did you make that up?
FLOYD:	Because I was scared. I didn't know what to do.
SENTENN:	John, I want you to look at the bottom of that page and each of these pages. Did you, in fact, sign those pages?
FLOYD:	Yes, sir. It's my signature. It was either sign it or get hit.
SENTENN:	Did you tell him you didn't want to sign it?
FLOYD:	Well, he told me what would happen if I didn't sign. He said, "If you don't give a statement . . ."
SENTENN:	What did he tell you would happen?
FLOYD:	He told me he'd kill me or beat me up so that I'd never be able to go back into the French Quarter.
SENTENN:	John, these are very serious charges lodged against you. Have you told the whole truth here today?
FLOYD:	Yes, sir.
SENTENN:	Is there anything in your testimony that you want to change, that you want to reflect on, any changes you want to make in anything that you testified to so far?
FLOYD:	Well, I had some more stuff that John Reilly said and all. I don't know whether it would do any good, about when he threatened me.
SENTENN:	But has everything that you told us been the truth?
FLOYD:	Yes, sir.

Plavnicky had to wait until after a recess—"to let Mr. Floyd rest for a while"—before cross-examining. Diane joined me in the big corridor outside the courtroom and gave my trembling body a needed hug.

"John, nobody believes those lies."

"It doesn't matter," I said.

But it did. Dark images, skittering rats, streaked in and out my mind. *Screw this goddam job,* I thought, not for the first time. *Screw the whole lash-up that makes me the bad guy.*

Crazy Johnny said I hit him. He said much worse. Right now I wanted to slam my fist into a wall.

"Nobody believes him," Diane repeated, softly.

"I don't know that." I looked into her eyes, searching her face. Anger and apprehension dominated my own.

"I guess you don't have much faith in me," she said.

Now I drew *her* close. My body still shook with rage.

"So many lies," she said.

"I could count them. Right from the start: one, Reilly wasn't in the room when we began, two—"

"Stop it, John."

I took Diane's hand and led her to a bench. We watched cops, spectators, witnesses, and court functionaries hurry back and forth. An old woman, homeless and looking for warmth, somehow had slipped upstairs. She asked us for a quarter.

"I think Mr. Sentenn is just terrible," Diane said, a few minutes later. "He knows John Floyd isn't telling the truth. He—"

"Sentenn's just doing his job, Di." I could accept it intellectually. "He's not making the charges, Floyd is. Johnny has to beat those confessions, and this is the only way. I don't think Sentenn enjoys it."

"Would you rather I go home?"

"Not now. Our side's coming to bat."

≡ 17 ≡

A lawsuit filed by Sentenn was one of several reasons why Floyd's trial took so long getting underway. The lawyer asked WVUE, Channel 8, ABC's New Orleans affiliate, for the videotape its cameraman took of Rice and me escorting Johnny on the Hollywood Walk. If Floyd was telling the truth, he'd resemble someone who went three rounds with Rocky Marciano.

Channel 8 refused to turn over the tape. Station management didn't want to become involved in police and criminal court matters. During the late 1960s and early 1970s, authorities attempted to obtain television films of demonstrations and later to require reporters to turn over notes of interviews. Numerous news organizations resisted, saying they couldn't meet First Amendment responsibilities if the public perceived them as appendages of law enforcement. No film footage to anybody. That's what Channel 8 told Sentenn.

He sued. He wasn't the FBI, he said, quite the opposite: he needed to investigate *police* abuses. More important, his client's freedom might very well depend on that tape.

It took eight months, but Sentenn won. Channel 8 had to turn over its footage showing the three of us on the Holly-

wood Walk. The unmarked Floyd seemed more spry than
either Mike or me.

Now David Plavnicky, armed with evidence he'd already
introduced, a picture of the three of us, plus mug shots taken
shortly after our arrival at Central Lockup (not a bruise on
Johnny, not a scratch), faced the defendant in open court.

PLAVNICKY: John, you say the police beat you up?
FLOYD: Yes, sir.
PLAVNICKY: Beat you bloody?
FLOYD: Yes.
PLAVNICKY: Now, after you—
FLOYD: Well, they didn't beat me bloody.
PLAVNICKY: Didn't you say you were bleeding?
FLOYD: Yes, I was bleeding. They didn't beat me
bloody. They busted my head open.
PLAVNICKY: To hear you describe it, it was a pretty se-
rious beating.
FLOYD: It was. They didn't bust my face up or
nothing like that, no.

This I wanted Diane to hear. According to Johnny, I kicked
him in the face, knocking him right off his chair, but didn't
"bust" anything.

PLAVNICKY: Did you explain to the doctor about your
injuries when you were booked?
FLOYD: They . . . it wouldn't have done any good.
PLAVNICKY: Do you remember they took your finger-
prints and a picture of you?
FLOYD: Yes, sir.
PLAVNICKY: Are you saying you never had the oppor-
tunity to tell anyone you had been beaten?
FLOYD: I was scared.

PLAVNICKY:	No one ever asked if you were injured?
FLOYD:	I told some people about it after I got locked up at C.C.C., but that was inmates.
PLAVNICKY:	And you remember they took your picture, don't you?
FLOYD:	Yes, sir, okay.
PLAVNICKY:	But you did not tell anyone at that time, look, the police just beat the hell out of me?
FLOYD:	I was afraid to, because they would probably beat me up again. I saw them beat people all night.

Sentenn, who had worked in the District Attorney's office, knew intimately what went on at the jail. I guessed he quickly came off the high he rode when he so deftly introduced the blood-type evidence—Johnny hadn't helped his own cause at all. Sentenn's labors had been Herculean: the suit against a rich TV station, the meticulous accumulation of the blood-type data, the fruitless searches for witnesses his client guaranteed existed—efforts far beyond what most criminal defendants received.

Well, too bad, I thought. I could appreciate the lawyer's efforts, sympathize with him at a personal level, but I didn't even want to *think* about Johnny back on the street.

Plavnicky turned his attention to the witnesses against Floyd.

PLAVNICKY:	Do you deny telling Mr. Reed that you killed the man at the Fairmont?
FLOYD:	I did not tell him that.
PLAVNICKY:	He just made it up?
FLOYD:	Yes, sir.
PLAVNICKY:	Why did Steven Edwards lie?

FLOYD:	He hates me, just like John Reilly. They got something in for me.
PLAVNICKY:	Do a lot of people hate you?
FLOYD:	Not all of them. I got some good friends in the French Quarter.
PLAVNICKY:	I can see they're filling up the courtroom.
WINSBERG:	Uh-uh, don't do that.

Judge Winsberg's stern tone reminded everyone to stick to testimony. Plavnicky, who normally dealt with a jury, simply forgot, or maybe he couldn't resist. At most murder trials the defendant produces *someone* as a character witness, at least one individual who can attest to a facet of his good nature. Crazy Johnny had a mother (his father was deceased), and thirty-two years under his belt, but the prosecutor knew no one would take the stand on his behalf.

Plavnicky attacked the bus-trip alibi for the Hines murder.

PLAVNICKY:	Mr. Floyd, you left San Francisco on the twentieth?
FLOYD:	Yes, sir.
PLAVNICKY:	And your testimony is it took you five days?
FLOYD:	Because I was laid over in Phoenix. We stopped in El Paso and San Antonio. I laid over there, and then in Houston.
PLAVNICKY:	Now, these tickets that are marked D-10, *in globo,* that your lawyer showed you. Do you have a ticket that shows the leg of your trip from Houston to New Orleans?
FLOYD:	No, sir.
PLAVNICKY:	All we have as to your arrival time in New Orleans is your word, correct?
FLOYD:	Yes, sir, and some people at the bar knew

	I was coming in. I called them from the station.
PLAVNICKY:	And who are these people?
FLOYD:	Carl knew I was coming in that day.
PLAVNICKY:	How many people at the bar knew this?
FLOYD:	It was four or five people in there, but I don't recall who all was there.
PLAVNICKY:	Do you know their names?
FLOYD:	One of them was named Ray at the Docks on Bourbon Street.
PLAVNICKY:	Who else?
FLOYD:	Carl the bartender. And a guy named J.C. who I worked with offshore. I can't think of the other guys.
PLAVNICKY:	Are any of these people here today?
FLOYD:	No, sir.
PLAVNICKY:	Have you made any effort to get in touch with these people?
FLOYD:	Well, I tried to get in touch with the bartender and the guy I lived with and Ray that runs the bar.
PLAVNICKY:	All of them?
FLOYD:	Strange, all of them had left town.

This line came from Johnny. Judge Winsberg wouldn't have tolerated it from Plavnicky. The prosecutor had latched onto a good thing and didn't want to let go.

PLAVNICKY:	Any of these people visit you in prison?
FLOYD:	I got letters from them.
PLAVNICKY:	They had addresses where you could write them?
FLOYD:	Yes, sir.
PLAVNICKY:	Did you write them?

FLOYD:	In Dallas, Texas. The guy I was living with, he moved to Fort Worth, Texas.
PLAVNICKY:	Did you write and ask him to come down?
FLOYD:	Well, he didn't want to get involved.
PLAVNICKY:	None of these—Ray, Carl, J.C.—or any of these other people, wanted to get involved?
FLOYD:	There's something going on funny somewhere. I don't know if John Reilly was threatening them or not.
PLAVNICKY:	Are you accusing John Reilly of scaring off these witnesses?
FLOYD:	I don't know it for a fact. Well, in my opinion, yes.
PLAVNICKY:	Do you know that for a fact? Can you testify under oath that John Reilly has done this?
FLOYD:	I don't know. Nobody said he done it, but in my opinion, yeah.

Witness-stand confessions may occur, but I've never seen one, except on TV. Plavnicky didn't aim for a confession. He believed it sufficient to hammer at the ludicrous stories Floyd told, and let Judge Winsberg decide. Hurling accusations at Crazy Johnny, and having him deny them, served no purpose; Sentenn asked Floyd if he were a murderer, and he answered no.

Floyd had been the last scheduled witness, but Plavnicky briefly reopened the prosecution's case to call John Reilly to the stand for a ritual denial of the accusations that he'd frightened witnesses. Reilly also testified that I hadn't beaten Crazy Johnny.

"You weren't in the room with them all the time, were you?" Sentenn said.

"I was right outside the door. I would have heard a beating."

"I asked, you weren't inside that room all the time, were you?"

"No, sir."

I believed Sentenn was flogging a dead horse because of the Channel 8 pictures and the mug shots.

Both sides, exhausted by the day and a half of concentrated intensity, rested their cases after Reilly's testimony. I asked Diane and Dantagnan—he took a busman's holiday to catch the Crazy Johnny show—to wait for me in the corridor and headed for the prosecution table. I disliked bothering Plavnicky, but already the suspense gnawed at me. I wanted the lawyer's estimate of how long we'd have to wait for court to reconvene.

"Probably ninety minutes," Plavnicky said. "Judge Winsberg won't take long."

"How does it look to you?"

"I think he's already made up his mind."

So did I. Before Reilly took the stand, Winsberg asked if the testimony would take long. "We've got a jury downstairs," he pointed out, indicating eagerness to apply himself to another case.

But *what* had made up his mind? The blood-type testimony? That he would likely take ninety minutes did not indicate uncertainty, only adequate time to review the evidence and make sure he didn't overlook anything.

"Are we going to win?" I asked.

Plavnicky shrugged. "It's a close one."

Cup after cup of coffee with Diane and Fred in the restaurant across from the Criminal Courts Building further jangled my nerves.

"Why don't you order a glass of milk, John?" Diane suggested, placing her hand over mine to arrest the cadence of my fingers drumming on the formica table top.

"Yeah, pace yourself," advised Fred. "You could worry up an ulcer before we get back in court."

"I'd bet my life Floyd butchered those two. The Hines case is crystal clear. Robinson—I was with Johnny when he confessed, and I know he did that one, too. But the water's all muddy."

"The type A blood," Dantagnan said.

"Worse than that. *We're* saying there's one killer. Geesus, think about those murder scenes. One animal did them both. If Winsberg decides Johnny didn't murder Robinson, he can say, 'Sorry, boys, but if he didn't do that one, you yourselves admit he didn't do the other.' Then Floyd walks."

"We just arrest 'em," Fred managed, not meaning it. "What comes after doesn't matter to us."

I sat on the aisle; to my right sat Diane, Fred, Mike Rice, John Reilly. True to prediction, Judge Winsberg took ninety minutes before reaching a decision.

David Plavnicky, directly in front of us, shuffled papers. Sentenn and Floyd, parallel to the prosecutor and to my left, leaned close to each other, conversing in whispers. I wondered, after all this time, what they could have to say.

Then he came briskly through a door at the front of the courtroom leading from his chambers, black robe flowing, his face—what? I couldn't read his features.

One thing is sure in a judge trial: no hung jury. We wouldn't have to go through this again. Unlike almost everything in human existence, where gray overrules the black and white, we were about to hear—no matter which way it went—a terrible finality.

Winsberg glanced down at some papers, then out over his

courtroom, reflexively prepared to call for quiet. But it was already quiet.

"Case Number 280-729, State of Louisiana versus John Floyd," Winsberg said in a clear, firm voice. He'd decide Robinson first. "The Court finds the defendant not guilty."

"My God," I said under my breath.

"How . . ." Diane said.

"Fuck!" Fred hissed.

Images assailed me, glimpsed in microseconds. Sentenn ever so slightly rearranging his bulk. Rice and Reilly wearing expressions hard and brooding. Plavnicky, trying to hide the hurt. Burning into my mind over all of it: Johnny smiling.

"Case Number 280-730, State of Louisiana versus John Floyd."

Hines.

I knew Winsberg would let Floyd go. *My own reasoning,* preached foolishly over and over to whomever asked ("Two murders—one killer"), *demanded* that he be let go.

Judge Winsberg again spoke clearly and firmly, for all of New Orleans to hear, for the ghost of Hines and for Robinson's, too. I counted Winsberg's words, knowing the sixth one would decide everything:

"The Court finds the defendant guilty."

Afterword

Rice and Reilly still serve on the NOPD, but Fred Dantagnan retired in 1987 to become chief of investigations for Dillmann/Guillot Associates, an investigative agency I head.

David Plavnicky entered private practice and today is a partner in the prestigious New Orleans law firm of Lee and Gibbons.

Judge Jerome Winsberg continues on the same Criminal Court bench, maintaining an enviable reputation for intelligence, fairness, and honesty.

John Floyd resides at the Louisiana State Penitentiary in Angola, doing a life sentence at hard labor, without possibility of parole for forty years. Twice the Louisiana Supreme Court upheld his conviction for the William Hines murder. Johnny professes to having undergone a profound religious experience, and today calls himself a born-again Christian.

Finally, the Rodney Robinson case gathers dust in Homicide's bottom drawer, technically an "open" investigation, but no officer who worked it believes the matter unsolved.

I visited Walter Sentenn during the course of writing this book, more than six years after the trial. I asked if he remembered the case, and particularly John Floyd.

"Remember him?" he said. "Of all the cases I've handled, his is the one that still bothers me." I could tell this wasn't just lawyer talk.

"We had those confessions." I hadn't come to argue with him.

"I never gave much credence to those."

"Floyd knew all those details. The Jack Daniel's bottle, the . . ."

"A good detective could feed him that information."

So that's how he felt.

Arguing, getting mad, would accomplish nothing. But the words came from my mouth anyway: "All those witnesses he couldn't find. That phony bus-ride alibi. If there'd been a grain of truth to any of it, you'd have found the proof."

"I warned him about those stories." The lawyer shook his head sadly.

We talked for twenty minutes. Sentenn lightened up a little. Maybe I hadn't beaten Johnny, after all.

But his mind couldn't let go of that type A blood. "Perhaps someone else was with Johnny that night. Maybe he was there, but another did the stabbing."

"No," I said, but Sentenn didn't listen.

"I couldn't live with it, you know, if Johnny had been a different kind of man. But I ask myself, and this is a horrible thing, is society not better off with him in jail?"

It was a down note I couldn't answer, couldn't buy, though the thought has crossed every cop's mind. Because I didn't share the lawyer's doubts, I dwelt instead on the positive, the good work that Mike, Fred, Reilly and I did. I wanted to think our labors were what Thomas Henry Huxley had in mind:

> We live in a world which is full of misery and ignorance, and the plain duty of each and all of us is to try to make the little corner he can influence somewhat less miserable and somewhat less ignorant than it was before he entered it.